Informing the legislative debate since 1914

Latin America: Terrorism Issues

Mark P. Sullivan
Specialist in Latin American Affairs

June S. Beittel
Analyst in Latin American Affairs

August 15, 2014

Congressional Research Service

7-5700

www.crs.gov

RS21049

Summary

U.S. attention to terrorism in Latin America intensified in the aftermath of the September 2001 terrorist attacks on New York and Washington, with an increase in bilateral and regional cooperation. In its 2013 *Country Reports on Terrorism* (issued in April 2014), the State Department maintained that the majority of terrorist attacks in the Western Hemisphere were committed by the Revolutionary Armed Forces of Colombia (FARC). The State Department asserted in that Latin American governments made modest improvements in their counterterrorism capabilities and border security, but that for some countries, corruption, weak government institutions, insufficient interagency cooperation, weak or nonexistent legislation, and a lack of resources impeded progress.

Over the past several years, policymakers have been concerned about Iran's increasing activities in Latin America. Concerns center on Iran's attempts to circumvent U.N. and U.S. sanctions, as well as on its ties to the radical Lebanon-based Islamic group Hezbollah. Both Iran and Hezbollah are reported to be linked to two bombings against Jewish targets in Argentina in the early 1990s. A June 2013 State Department report to Congress on Iran's activities in Latin America asserted that Iran's influence in the region is waning. Some critics maintain that the State Department is playing down the threat posed by Iran in the region, while others contend that while Iran's involvement in the region is a concern, its level and significance are being exaggerated. As in past years, the State Department's 2013 terrorism report maintained that "there were no known operational cells of either Al Qaeda or Hezbollah in the hemisphere," but noted that "ideological sympathizers in South America and the Caribbean continued to provide financial and ideological support to those and other terrorist groups in the Middle East and South Asia."

Cuba has remained on the State Department's list of state sponsors of terrorism since 1982 pursuant to Section 6(j) of the Export Administration Act. Both Cuba and Venezuela are on the State Department's annual list of countries determined to be not cooperating fully with U.S. antiterrorism efforts pursuant to Section 40A of the Arms Export Control Act. U.S. officials have expressed concerns over the past several years about Venezuela's lack of cooperation on antiterrorism efforts, its relations with Iran, and the involvement of senior Venezuelan officials in supporting the drug and weapons trafficking activities of the FARC. In recent years, however, improved Venezuelan-Colombian relations have resulted in closer cooperation on antiterrorism and counternarcotics efforts and border security.

Legislative Initiatives

In the 112th Congress, several legislative initiatives were introduced and several oversight hearings were held related to terrorism issues in the Western Hemisphere regarding Mexico, Venezuela, and the activities of Iran and Hezbollah in the region. Most significantly, the 112th Congress enacted the Countering Iran in the Western Hemisphere Act of 2012 (P.L. 112-220) in December 2012, which required the Administration within 180 days to conduct an assessment and present "a strategy to address Iran's growing hostile presence and activity in the Western Hemisphere."

The 113th Congress has continued its oversight of terrorism concerns in the Western Hemisphere, especially the activities of Iran and Hezbollah. The State Department assessment of Iranian activities in the region and the U.S. strategy to address them was the subject of two oversight hearings, and other oversight hearing have been held touching on terrorism issues in the region (see "113th Congress" below). In terms of legislative initiatives, two have been introduced in the 113th Congress related to Cuba: H.R. 1917 (Rush), introduced May 9, 2013, would among its provisions rescind any determination of the Secretary of State in effect on the date of enactment of the Act that Cuba has repeatedly provided support for acts of international terrorism; H.Res. 262 (King), introduced June 14, 2013, would call for the immediate extradition or rendering to the United States of all fugitives from justice who are receiving safe harbor in Cuba in order to escape prosecution or confinement for criminal offenses in the United States. For a number of years, the State Department has noted in its annual terrorism report Cuba's harboring of fugitives wanted in the United States.

Contents

Figures

Tables

Contacts

Recent Developments

On July 23, 2014, Aruban authorities detained retired Venezuelan General Hugo Carvajal at the request of the U.S. government, but he was released on July 27 after Dutch officials ruled that Carvajal was protected by diplomatic immunity. The Treasury Department had sanctioned Carvajal in 2008 for helping Colombia's FARC with weapons and narcotics trafficking. (See **Table 1** on Venezuela and FARC-related sanctions, below.)

On May 12, 2014, Secretary of State John Kerry issued an annual determination and certification, pursuant to Section 40A of the Arms Export Control Act, that Cuba and Venezuela "are not cooperating fully with United States antiterrorism efforts." Other countries on the annual list are Eritrea, Iran, North Korea, and Syria. (See sections on Cuba and Venezuela, below.)

On May 15, 2014, an Argentine federal court declared unconstitutional an agreement with Iran that had been reached in January 2013 to jointly investigate the 1994 bombing of the Argentine-Israeli Mutual Association (AMIA) in Buenos Aires. The bombing killed 85 people and allegedly has been linked to Iran and Hezbollah. The government of President Cristina Fernández de Kirchner maintained that it would appeal the ruling to Argentina's Supreme Court. (See **Table 2** on the AMIA bombing investigation.)

On April 30, 2014, the State Department issued its *Country Reports on Terrorism 2013*, which stated, as in past years, that the majority of terrorist attacks in the Western Hemisphere were committed by the FARC. The report also stated that "Iran's influence in the Western Hemisphere remained a concern," but that "due to strong sanctions imposed on the country by the United States and the European Union, Iran has been unable to expand its economic and political ties in Latin America." (The State Department report is available at http://www.state.gov/j/ct/rls/crt/2013/index.htm)

On February 26, 2014 and March 13, 2014, General John F. Kelly, Commander of the U.S. Southern Command (SOUTHCOM), presented SOUTHCOM's 2014 posture statement to the House and Senate Armed Services Committees respectively. Kelly maintained that "Iran's involvement in the Western Hemisphere is a mater for concern," and that he remains concerned about the presence of Hezbollah in the region. (See "U.S. Policy and Sanctions Related to Iran in Latin America" below.)

On February 20-21, 2014, the Inter-American Committee on Terrorism (CICTE) of the Organization of American States held its annual session in Washington, D.C. CICTE members focused attention on: how to counter criminal activities that may exacerbate the threat of terrorism, such as money laundering and trafficking in drugs, arms, and people; and how to strengthen criminal justice responses to acts of terrorism. (See "Increased Regional Cooperation Since 9/11" below.)

On February 4, 2014, the House Committee on Foreign Affairs, Subcommittee on Terrorism, Nonproliferation, and Trade, held a hearing on "Terrorist Groups in Latin America: The Changing Landscape" focusing on efforts to combat the Shining Path in Peru and the FARC in Colombia, as well as concerns about the activities of Hezbollah in the region.

Terrorism in Latin America: U.S. Concerns

Over the years, the United States has been concerned about threats to Latin American and Caribbean nations from various terrorist or insurgent groups that have attempted to influence or overthrow elected governments. Although Latin America has not been the focal point in the war on terrorism, countries in the region have struggled with domestic terrorism for decades and international terrorist groups have at times used the region as a battleground to advance their causes.

The State Department's annual *Country Reports on Terrorism* highlights U.S. concerns about terrorist threats around the world, including in Latin America. As in reports in recent years, the 2013 report (issued in April 2014) maintained that the majority of terrorist attacks in the Western Hemisphere were committed by the Revolutionary Armed Forces of Colombia (FARC). The State Department asserted in the 2013 report that "transnational criminal organizations continued to pose a more significant threat to the region than transnational terrorism" and that "most countries in the region made efforts to investigate possible connections with terrorist organizations."

U.S. policymakers have expressed concerns over the past several years about Iran's deepening relations with several Latin American countries, especially Venezuela, and its activities in the region. The 2013 terrorism report noted that "Iran's influence in the Western Hemisphere remained a concern," but noted that "due to strong sanctions imposed on the country by the United States and the European Union, Iran has been unable to expand its economic and political ties in Latin America." This correlates with a June 2013 State Department report to Congress pursuant to the Countering Iran in the Western Hemisphere Act of 2012 (P.L. 112-220), which described Iranian influence in Latin America and the Caribbean as "waning." Likewise in March 2013, General John Kelly, the head of the U.S. Southern Command (SOUTHCOM), testified before Congress that "Iran is struggling to maintain influence in the region," and that "its efforts to cooperate with a small set of countries with interests that are inimical to the United States are waning."

One of the main concerns about Iran's increasing relations with the region is its ties to Hezbollah, the radical Lebanon-based Islamic group that the Department of State designated a Foreign Terrorist Organization in 1997. While the State Department asserted in its 2013 terrorism report that there were no known operational cells of either Hezbollah or Al Qaeda or in the hemisphere, it noted that "ideological sympathizers in South America and the Caribbean continued to provide financial and moral support to those and other terrorist groups in the Middle East and South Asia." In particular, the State Department noted that the tri-border area of Argentina, Brazil, and Paraguay "continued to be an important regional nexus of arms, narcotics, and human trafficking; counterfeiting; pirated goods; and money laundering—all potential funding sources of terrorist organizations."

There has been significant U.S. concern in recent years about the increasing and brutal violence of Mexico's drug trafficking organizations, with more than 70,000 drug trafficking-related deaths in Mexico from 2007 through 2013. In response to some concerns that these criminal organizations may be adopting terrorist tactics, the State Department asserted in its 2010 and 2011 and terrorism reports that there was no evidence of ties between Mexican criminal groups and terrorist groups. The 2012 terrorism report stated "there was no evidence that these criminal organizations had political or ideological motivations, aside from seeking to maintain the impunity with which they conduct their criminal activities." The 2013 terrorism report asserted that there were "no known international terrorist organizations operating in Mexico," and "no evidence that any terrorist group has targeted U.S. citizens in Mexican territory."

In terms of Latin American countries' abilities to combat terrorism, the State Department maintained in the 2013 terrorism report that Latin American governments "made modest improvements to their counterterrorism capabilities and their border security." The State Department also noted in the report, however, that "corruption, weak government institutions, insufficient interagency cooperation, weak or nonexistent legislation, and a lack of resources remained the primary causes for the lack of significant progress" in some countries in the region.

Since 1982, Cuba has been on the State Department's state sponsors of terrorism list pursuant to Section 6(j) of the Export Administration Act (EAA) of 1979. The state sponsors of terrorism list is not an annual list. Rather, countries remain on the list until either the President or Congress takes action to remove a country. The EAA sets forth procedures for the President to remove a country from the list. In addition, the State Department currently lists two Latin American countries—Cuba and Venezuela—on its annual list of countries that are not "cooperating fully with United States antiterrorism efforts" pursuant to Section 40A of the Arms Export Control Act. The most recent annual determination was made in May 2014.[1]

Colombia[2]

Three violent Colombian groups are designated by the Secretary of State as Foreign Terrorist Organizations (FTOs). Two of these, the leftist Revolutionary Armed Forces of Colombia (FARC) and the leftist National Liberation Army (ELN), were both designated in 1997, and are active guerrilla groups. A third group, the rightist paramilitary United Self-Defense Forces of Colombia (AUC), was designated an FTO in 2001, but the group has been demobilized for seven years.

The State Department's 2013 terrorism report maintains that the number of terrorist incidents in the country—perpetrated largely by the FARC (Colombia's largest active terrorist group) and the ELN—decreased by 7% in 2013 to 830, even though the number of attacks against infrastructure increased by 46% during the year. According to the report, the FARC reportedly focused on low-cost high-impact attacks, such as the launching of mortars at police stations or the military, explosive devices placed near roads or paths, and sniper attacks. Terrorist attacks on infrastructure by the FARC and ELN were particularly focused on oil pipelines and equipment.

The FARC, a leftist guerrilla group heavily involved in drug production and trafficking, was established in the early 1960s. Over the past several years, the FARC has been weakened significantly by the government's military campaign against it. In March 2008, the military killed the group's second in command, Raúl Reyes, during a raid on a FARC camp in Ecuador. In May 2008, the FARC admitted that its long-time leader, Manuel Marulanda, had died of a heart attack in March. In July 2008, a Colombian military operation in the southeastern province of Guaviare rescued 15 long-held hostages, including three U.S. defense contractors (held since February 2003) and a prominent Colombian Senator and presidential candidate. The Colombian military

---

[1] Department of State, "Determination and Certification Under Section 40A of the Arms Export Control Act," 79 *Federal Register* 32357, June 4, 2014.

[2] For additional information, see CRS Report R42982, *Peace Talks in Colombia*, and CRS Report IN10024, *Colombia's 2014 Elections: Referendum on the Peace Process*, by June S. Beittel. For background, see CRS Report RL32250, *Colombia: Background, U.S. Relations, and Congressional Interest*, by June S. Beittel.

dealt a significant blow to the terrorist group in September 2010 when it killed a top military commander, Victor Julio Suárez (aka "Mono Joyoy") in a bombing raid on his camp in a mountainous region of Meta department in central Colombia. In November 2011, the Colombian military killed the FARC's leader, Alfonso Cano, in a bombing raid in the department of Cauca in southwestern Colombia. In September 2012, a top FARC commander, Danilo García, was killed in a military raid in the northern department of Norte de Santander. In August 2013, a Colombian Air Force raid killed the leader of the FARC's 57th Front in Chocó department bordering Panama. In July 2014, the FARC's commander of its 30th Front, who also allegedly was the group's drug trafficking boss on the country's Pacific coast, was captured.[3]

Despite the military campaign against it, the FARC is estimated to have a strength of around about 8,000-9,000 fighters, operating in various locations throughout Colombia. The group has been responsible for terrorist attacks, including the destruction of infrastructure, kidnapping, extortion, and has now diversified into illegal mining.[4] In the aftermath of the killing of FARC leader Alfonso Cano in November 2011, the FARC chose Rodrigo Londoño, also known as Timoleón Jiménez or Timochenko, as its new leader.

In August 2012, the Colombian government of President Juan Manuel Santos announced that it had begun exploratory peace talks with the FARC. Formal talks began in Norway in October 2012, and have continued in Cuba. To date, the two sides have reached agreements on three of the five substantive agenda items: land and rural development, political participation, and resolving the problem of illicit drugs. Remaining items are a framework for ending the conflict (including a cessation of hostilities and the handover of weapons) and compensation for victims. President Santos was reelected to a second term in June 2014 and primarily based his campaign on a peace platform to continue the peace negotiations. In late July 2014, President Santos strongly criticized continued FARC terrorist attacks and warned that such behavior could jeopardize the peace talks.[5]

The ELN, a Marxist-Leninist group formed in 1965, reportedly has a membership of around 2,000 fighters with diminished resources and reduced offensive capability, but has continued to undertake attacks and inflict casualties. In 2013, the group increased its attacks on oil pipelines and equipment and such attacks have continued in 2014, including a major attack on August 12 on a pipeline in the eastern department of Arauca bordering Venezuela (see **Figure 1**).The ELN has been located largely in the rural and mountainous areas of northern, northeastern, and southwestern Colombia, and also in the eastern border region with Venezuela where reportedly the group has its base. In June 2014, the ELN and the Colombian government confirmed that they were engaged in exploratory peace talks, but official talks have not yet begun. In recent years, the ELN has been involved in joint attacks with the FARC. Like the FARC, the group derives its funding from drug trafficking as well as from kidnapping and extorting oil and gas companies.

The AUC was formed in 1997 as a loosely affiliated paramilitary group targeting leftist guerrillas. It carried out numerous political killings and kidnappings and was heavily involved in the drug trade. More than 32,000 AUC members demobilized between 2003 and 2006, and the group's

---

[3] Camilo Mejia Giraldo, "Arrest of FARC's Pacific Narco Boss Shines Light on Rebel Drug Ops," *InSight Crime, Organized Crime in the Americas*, July 22, 2014.

[4] Historically the FTO has been responsible for numerous kidnappings, but it claimed to end the practice in early 2012 in an overture to open peace talks with the Colombian government.

[5] Peter Murphy, "Colombia President Says 'Demented' FARC Attacks Could End Peace Talks," *Reuters*, July 29, 2014.

paramilitary chiefs stepped down. In the aftermath of the AUC's demobilization, however, former AUC paramilitaries continued to engage in criminal activities, mostly drug trafficking, in new criminal groups (known as BACRIM, *Bandas Criminales*)—reportedly some 30 such criminal groups were established. Human rights groups maintain that these successor groups to the paramilitaries have been responsible for widespread abuses against civilians.[6] The largest and most powerful BACRIM that has emerged is known as Los Urabeños (also referred to as the Gaitanista Self-Defense Forces),which is heavily involved in cocaine trafficking as well as arms trafficking, money laundering, extortion, gold mining, human trafficking, gambling, and prostitution.[7]

Colombian FTOs in Neighboring Countries

Colombian terrorist groups have continued to use the territory of several of Colombia's neighbors—Ecuador, Panama, and Venezuela—according to the State Department's terrorism report (**Figure 1**). Border areas with Venezuela, Panama, and Ecuador reportedly are used for incursions into Colombia and Venezuelan and Ecuadorian territory is reportedly used for safe haven, according to the report.

While Ecuador's relations with Colombia became tense in the aftermath of Colombia's March 2008 military raid on a FARC camp in Ecuador's Sucumbios province (see **Figure 1**), Ecuador's military subsequently increased the number of operations against the FARC in its northern border region. Under Colombian President Santos, who took office in August 2010, the two countries made progress in improving bilateral relations, and restored diplomatic relations in December 2010. The 2013 terrorism report maintained that improved relations between Colombia and Ecuador have led to increased cooperation on law enforcement issues.

In Panama, a small number of FARC members from the group's 57th Front operated in the country's Darien province bordering Colombia for a number of years, using the area as a safe haven. Panama's government has stepped up its efforts in recent years to confront this presence by patrolling the province and conducting raids against FARC camps. Panama has cooperated closely with Colombia to secure its border, and in June 2013 agreed to establish a joint operations base on the common border.[8] In July 2013, then-Panamanian President Ricardo Martinelli contended that Panama's security forces had 100% control of Panamanian territory in the Darien border area, compared to 2009 when the FARC controlled 25% of Darien.[9] The State Department's 2013 terrorism report notes that Panama's National Border Service (SENAFRONT) undertook operations in 2013 that degraded the FARC's capabilities in Panama so that they cannot maintain a permanent presence. Nevertheless, the FARC reportedly continues to use

---

[6] See for example, Human Rights Watch, *World Report 2014: Colombia*, available at http://www.hrw.org/world-report/2014/country-chapters/colombia

[7] President Obama identified Los Urabeños as a Specially Designated Narcotics Trafficker pursuant to the Foreign Narcotics Kingpin Designation Act in May 2013, and the Treasury Department froze the assets of 17 leaders and criminal associates of Los Urabeños along with six business in Colombia pursuant to the Kingpin Act. See U.S. Department of the Treasury, "Treasury Sanctions Los Urabeños Leadership," July 23, 2014; "The Urabeños—The Criminal Hybrid," *InSight Crime, Organized Crime in the Americas*, May 2, 2014.

[8] "Panama and Colombia Announce Construction of a Joint Base in Darién," *Forecast International Defense Intelligence Newsletters*, June 24, 2013.

[9] "Afirma President Martinelli Que Panamá Está Libre de las FARC," *Agencia Mexicana de Noticias*, July 1, 2013.

Panamanian territory for the transit of illicit drugs. In 2014, there have been several confrontations between the FARC and Panama's SENAFRONT, including an incident in July in which two alleged FARC members were killed.[10]With regard to Venezuela, both the FARC and ELN have long been reported to have a presence in Venezuelan territory, and the United States has imposed sanctions on several current and former Venezuelan government and military officials for providing support to the FARC. (Also see section on "Venezuela" below.) As described in the State Department's 2010 terrorism report, the previous Colombian government of President Álvaro Uribe publicly accused the Venezuelan government several times of harboring members of the FARC and ELN in its territory.[11] In July 2010, the Uribe government presented evidence at the OAS of FARC training camps in Venezuela. In response, Venezuela suspended diplomatic relations in July 2010, yet less than three weeks later new Colombian President Juan Manuel Santos met with then-Venezuelan President Chávez and the two leaders agreed to reestablish diplomatic relations and to improve military patrols along their common border.

Since then, Venezuelan-Colombian relations on border security have improved, with ongoing high-level dialogue. At times, Venezuela has captured and returned to Colombia several members of the FARC and ELN. For example, in 2012, Colombian-Venezuelan security cooperation led to the capture of wanted Colombian drug kingpin Daniel Barrera (alias "El Loco") in September. Barrera was captured in the Venezuelan border state of Táchira in a joint operation and had allegedly served as a bridge between the FARC, rightwing paramilitaries, and some of Colombia's largest drug trafficking organizations for two decades.[12] In December 2013, Venezuelan captured FARC commander Reinel Guzman in the bordering state of Apure.[13]

As noted above, the State Department's 2013 terrorism report maintained that the FARC and ELN use Venezuela for incursions into Colombia and that Venezuelan territory is used for safe haven, with individuals linked to both the FARC and ELN present in Venezuela. Moreover, the terrorism report also noted that Venezuela has taken no action against senior Venezuelan government officials sanctioned by the U.S. Treasury Department for directly supporting the narcotics and arms trafficking activities of the FARC (see **Table 1**.) Elements of the Venezuela military believed to be most deeply involved in the drug trade are concentrated along the border with Colombia in the Venezuelan states of Apure, Zulia, and Táchira (see **Figure 1**).[14]

---

[10] Mimi Yagoub, "Panama Police Clash with Colombia's FARC in Cross Border Drug Corridor," *InSight Crime, Organized Crime in the Americas*, July 15, 2014.

[11] U.S. Department of State, Country Reports on Terrorism 2010," August 18, 2011.

[12] William Neuman and Jenny Carolina González, "Unlikely Joint Effort by U.S. and Venezuela Leads to a Drug Lord's Arrest," *Washington Post*, September 23, 2012; "Narco's Capture Boon for Colombia & Venezuela," *LatinNews Daily Report*, September 19, 2012.

[13] "Capturan en Venezuela a Líder de las FARC, Rafael Gutiérrez," *Diario las Américas*, December 18, 2013.

[14] "Cartel de los Soles," *InSight Crime, Organized Crime in the Americas,* 2012.

Figure 1. Colombia and Neighboring Countries

Source: CRS.

Notes: The map shows Colombia's departments and the bordering departments, provinces, and states of neighboring Ecuador, Peru, Brazil, Venezuela, and Panama.

Cuba[15]

The Department of State, pursuant to Section 6(j) of the Export Administration Act (EAA) of 1979, has included Cuba among its list of states sponsoring terrorism since 1982 (the other states currently on the list are Iran, Sudan, and Syria). Communist Cuba had a history of supporting revolutionary movements and governments in Latin America and Africa, but in 1992, then Cuban leader Fidel Castro said that his country's support for insurgents abroad was a thing of the past. Most analysts accept that Cuba's policy generally did change, largely because the breakup of the Soviet Union resulted in the loss of billions in subsidies. As noted above, Cuba is also on the State Department's annual list of countries determined to be not cooperating fully with U.S. antiterrorism efforts pursuant to Section 40A of the Arms Export Control Act.

Cuba's retention on the terrorism list has been questioned by some observers. In general, those who support keeping Cuba on the list point to the government's history of supporting terrorist acts and armed insurgencies in Latin America and Africa. They point to the government's continued hosting of members of foreign terrorist organizations and U.S. fugitives from justice. Critics of retaining Cuba on the terrorism list maintain that it is a holdover of the Cold War. They argue that domestic political considerations keep Cuba on the terrorism list, while North Korea and Libya (before the overthrow of the Qadhafi regime) were removed, and maintain that Cuba's presence on the list diverts U.S. attention from struggles against serious terrorist threats.

In its 2013 terrorism report (issued in April 2014), the State Department stated that Cuba has long provided safe haven to members of the Basque Fatherland and Liberty (ETA) and the Revolutionary Armed Forces of Colombia (FARC). The report noted, however, that Cuba's ties to ETA have become more distant and that about eight of the two dozen ETA members in Cuba were relocated with the cooperation of the Spanish government. With regard to the FARC, the terrorism report noted that throughout 2012, the Cuban government supported and hosted peace negotiations between the FARC and the Colombian government. As in its 2011 and 2012 reports, the State Department stated in the 2013 terrorism report that "there was no indication that the Cuban government provided weapons or paramilitary training to terrorist groups."

Another issue noted in the 2013 terrorism report that has been mentioned for many years in the annual report is Cuba's harboring of fugitives wanted in the United States. The report maintained that Cuba provided such support as housing, food ration books, and medical care for these individuals. U.S. fugitives from justice in Cuba include convicted murderers and numerous hijackers, most of whom entered Cuba in the 1970s and early 1980s.[16] For example, Joanne Chesimard, also known as Assata Shakur, was added to the FBI's Most Wanted Terrorist list on May 2, 2013. Chesimard was part of militant group known as the Black Liberation Army. In 1977, she was convicted for the 1973 murder of a New Jersey State Police officer and sentenced to life in prison. Chesimard escaped from prison in 1979, and according to the FBI, lived underground before fleeing to Cuba in 1984.[17] In addition to Chesimard and other fugitives from

---

[15] For additional information, see CRS Report R43024, *Cuba: U.S. Policy and Issues for the 113th Congress*, by Mark P. Sullivan. For background information, see archived CRS Report RL32251, *Cuba and the State Sponsors of Terrorism List* (August 22, 2006).

[16] U.S. Department of State, *Country Reports on Terrorism 2007*, April 30, 2008.

[17] FBI, Most Wanted Terrorists, Joanne Deborah Chesimard, Poster, at http://www.fbi.gov/wanted/wanted_terrorists/joanne-deborah-chesimard/view.

the past, a number of U.S. fugitives from justice wanted for Medicare and other types of insurance fraud reportedly have fled to Cuba in recent years.[18]

Cuba in recent years has returned wanted fugitives to the United States on a case by case basis. For example, in 2011, U.S. Marshals picked up a husband and wife in Cuba who were wanted for a 2010 murder in New Jersey,[19] while in April 2013, Cuba returned a Florida couple who had allegedly kidnapped their own children (who had been in the custody of the mother's parents) and fled to Havana.[20] In November 2013, William Potts, an American citizen who had hijacked an airplane from New Jersey to Havana in 1984, returned to the United States to face air-piracy charges; he had served 14 years in a Cuban jail for his crime.[21] On July 17, 2014, Potts was sentenced to 20 years in jail by a U.S. federal judge in Florida.

Cuba, however, has generally refused to render to U.S. justice any fugitive judged by Cuba to be "political," such as Chesimard, who they believe could not receive a fair trial in the United States. Moreover, Cuba in the past has responded to U.S. extradition requests by stating that approval would be contingent upon the United States returning wanted Cuban criminals from the United States. These include the return of Luis Posada Carriles, whom Cuba accused of plotting the 1976 bombing of a Cuban jet that killed 73 people (see further discussion of Posada below). Cuba had also long sought the return of a militant Cuban exile, Orlando Bosch, whom Cuba also accused of responsibility for the 1976 airplane bombing (Bosch died in Florida in 2011).

In the 113th Congress, a House resolution was introduced June 14, 2013, H.Res. 262 (King), that would call for the immediate extradition or rendering to the United States of convicted felon William Morales and all fugitives from justice who are receiving safe harbor in Cuba in order to escape prosecution or confinement for criminal offenses in the United States. In 1978, Morales, a member of the Puerto Rican militant group known as the Armed Forces of National Liberation (FALN), was maimed by a bomb he was making that blew off nine of his fingers. He was convicted in New York on weapons charges and sentenced to 89 years in prison, but in 1979 he escaped from New York's Bellevue Hospital and fled to Mexico, where he reportedly worked for a revolutionary group. In 1983, Morales was imprisoned in Mexico after a shootout with police; once his sentence was completed in 1988, Morales was allowed to go to Cuba, where he reportedly remains.[22]

The 2012 terrorism report noted that Cuba became a member of the Financial Action Task Force of South America (GAFISUD), a regional group associated with the multilateral Financial Action Task Force (FATF), in December 2012. As such, Cuba has committed to adopting and implementing the 40 recommendations of the FATF pertaining to international standards on

---

[18] For example, see The United States Attorney's Office, Southern District of Florida, "Thirty-three Defendants Charged in Staged Automobile Accident Scheme," Press Release, May 16, 201; Legal Forum, Experts: Florida Couple May Not Be Welcome in Cuba," *Naples Daily News*, April 9, 2013; and Jay Weaver, "FBI Struggling to Catch Dozens of Fraud Fugitives Hiding in Cuba," *Miami Herald*, July 16, 2011.

[19] George Mast, "Murder Suspects Caught in Cuba," *Courier-Post* (New Jersey), September 30, 2011.

[20] Paul Haven and Peter Orsi, "Cuba Says It Will Give U.S. Florida Couple Who Allegedly Kidnapped Children," *Associated Press*, April 9, 2013.

[21] Zachary Fagenson, "Ex-Black Panther Sentenced to 20 Years for 1980s Hijacking," *Reuters*, July 17, 2014.

[22] James Anderson, "Living in Exile, Maimed Guerrilla Maintains Low-Key Profile in Cuba," *Fort Worth Star-Telegram*, January 16, 2000; Vanessa Bauza, "FBI's Fugitive Is Cuba's Political Refugee," *South Florida Sun-Sentinel*, May 26, 2002; Mary Jordan, "Fugitives Sought by U.S. Find a Protector in Cuba," *Washington Post*, September 2, 2002.

combating money laundering and the financing of terrorism and proliferation.[23] Cuba is scheduled to undergo a GAFISUD mutual evaluation in 2014 examining its compliance and implementation of the FATF recommendations.[24]

As set forth in Section 6(j) of the Export Administration Act, a country's retention on the terrorism list may be rescinded in two ways. The first option is for the President to submit a report to Congress certifying that there has been a fundamental change in the leadership and policies of the government and that the government is not supporting acts of international terrorism and is providing assurances that it will not support such acts in the future. The second option is for the President to submit a report to Congress, at least 45 days in advance justifying the rescission and certifying that the government has not provided any support for international terrorism during the preceding six months, and has provided assurances that it will not support such acts in the future.

Another potential option to remove Cuba from the state sponsors of terrorism list is set forth in H.R. 1917 (Rush) introduced in the 113th Congress. Section 10 of the bill would rescind any determination of the Secretary of State in effect on the date of enactment of the Act that Cuba has repeatedly provided support for acts of international terrorism. The bill references not only Section 6(j) of the Export Administration Act (50 U.S.C. appendix 2504(j)), but also Section 620A of the Foreign Assistance Act of 1961 (22 U.S.C. 2371) and Section 40 of the Arms Export Control Act (22 U.S.C. 2780).

In February 2013, a press report claimed that high ranking State Department officials concluded that Cuba should not be on the state sponsors of terrorism list, but State Department officials contend that the report was incorrect and that there are no current plans to remove Cuba from the list.[25] Some observers maintain that Cuba's role in facilitating Colombia's peace talks could ultimately be a factor in removing Cuba from the list.

Cuba has been the target of various terrorist incidents over the years. As noted above, in 1976, a Cuban plane was bombed, killing 73 people. In 1997, there were almost a dozen bombings in the tourist sector in Havana in which an Italian businessman was killed and several others were injured. In November 2000, four anti-Castro activists were arrested in Panama for a plot to kill Fidel Castro. The four stood trial in March 2004 and were sentenced on weapons charges to prison terms ranging from seven to eight years. In late August 2004, Panamanian President Mireya Moscoso pardoned the four men before the end of her presidential term. One of the men, Luis Posada Carriles (a nationalized Venezuelan citizen originally from Cuba), as noted above, is also alleged to be involved in the 1976 Cuban airline bombing as well as the series of bombings in Havana in 1997.[26]

Posada entered the United States illegally in 2005. In subsequent removal proceedings, an immigration judge found that Posada could not be removed to Cuba or Venezuela because of

---

[23] Financial Action Task Force, International Standards on Combating Money Laundering and the Financing of Terrorism & Proliferation, The FATF Recommendations," February 2012, available at http://www.gafisud.info/documentos/eng/40_Recommendations.pdf

[24] See the website of the GAFISUD at http://www.gafisud.info/eng-index.php

[25] Bryan Bender, "Talk Grows of Taking Cuba Off Terror List," *Boston Globe*, February 21, 2013; U.S. Department of State, Daily Press Briefing, February 21, 2013.

[26] Frances Robles, "An Old Foe of Castro Looks Back on His Fight," *Miami Herald*, September 4, 2003.

concerns that he would face torture, and he was thereafter permitted to remain in the United States pending such time as he could be transferred to a different country. Posada subsequently applied for naturalization to become a U.S. citizen. This application was denied, and criminal charges were brought against him for allegedly false statements made in his naturalization application and interview. Although a federal district court dismissed the indictment in 2007, its ruling was reversed by an appellate court in 2008. In April 2009, the United States filed a superseding indictment, which included additional criminal charges based for allegedly make false statements made by Posada in immigration removal proceedings concerning his involvement in the 1997 Havana bombings. Posada's trial began in January 2011 and he ultimately was acquitted of the perjury charges in April 2011.[27]

Mexico[28]

Mexico is a major transit point for the lucrative cocaine trade and a major source and trafficking country for marijuana, methamphetamine, and heroin. This highly lucrative market has generated fierce competition within and between the drug trafficking organizations (DTOs) to control trafficking routes into the United States and for a share of the growing internal drug market inside Mexico. Violence perpetrated by the DTOs in Mexico began to increase significantly in 2007 and many analysts characterized the level of brutality as unprecedented for the country. From 2007 through 2013, there were more than 70,000 organized crime-related deaths in Mexico. The Mexican government reports that homicides decreased by about 9% in 2013, but during the same period, the number of reported kidnapping and extortion cases increased about almost 21% and 11%, respectively.[29]

The upsurge in crime in Mexico, spawned by the illicit drug trade, which has broadened into many other types of crime, and the brutality of the tactics led some analysts to liken certain DTO activities to those of terrorists or armed insurgents.[30] DTO-related violence has involved brazen and high profile crimes such as car bombings, deadly blockades, use of grenades, and at times even indiscriminate attacks involving civilians, although much of the violence has been between DTO rivals as well as engagement with Mexican security forces.[31] Homicides attributed to the DTOs have included beheadings, hangings, dismemberment of victims' bodies, and torture. The

---

[27] For additional information, see "Background on Luis Posada Carriles," CRS Congressional Distribution Memorandum, December 8, 2010, prepared by Mark P. Sullivan, Specialist in Latin American Affairs, and Michael John Garcia, Legislative Attorney. Available from the authors.

[28] For further background, see CRS Report R41349, *U.S.-Mexican Security Cooperation: The Mérida Initiative and Beyond*, by Clare Ribando Seelke and Kristin Finklea, and CRS Report R41576, *Mexico's Drug Trafficking Organizations: Source and Scope of the Violence*, by June S. Beittel and CRS Report R42917, *Mexico: Background and U.S. Relations*, by Clare Ribando Seelke.

[29] U.S. Department of State, *2014 International Narcotics Control Strategy Report*, Volume 1, March 2014.

[30] See, for example, Robert J. Bunker and John P. Sullivan, "Cartel Evolution Revisited: Third Phase Cartel Potentials and Alternative Futures in Mexico," *Small Wars & Insurgencies*, vol. 21, no. 1 (March 2010).

[31] Incidents of indiscriminate attacks on civilians have been quite rare, although there have been a number of harrowing cases of alleged mistaken identity including mass slayings as well as an increasing number of innocent bystanders killed in violent DTO shootouts. Two incidents stand out. One is an attack when grenades were thrown into a crowd gathered for Independence Day festivities in Morelia in September 2008, and the other the firebombing of a casino in Monterrey, Nuevo León in August 2011. The grenade attack, which killed eight, was widely condemned by the major drug trafficking groups and no group took credit for it. It appears to be a one-time event that has not been repeated. The casino firebombing, with a death toll of more than fifty, has been linked to Los Zetas and appears to be an example of organized crime's involvement in corruption and extortion. See Tracy Wilkinson, "Suspect Says Mexico Casino Fire Set Over Unpaid Extortion Money," *Los Angeles Times*, August 29, 2011.

DTO actions, however, while indeed carried out to instill fear and generate compliance, are not paired with terrorist political motivation or intent. Rather, their actions are motivated by a ruthless pursuit of profit. The organizations lack a religious or political ideology with the goal of destroying the government or undermining legitimate authority, except to continue to neutralize the government's efforts to curtail their illicit businesses.

Some analysts contend that characterizing the DTOs as terrorists misconstrues the problem. University of Pittsburgh Professor Phil Williams observes that the violence in Mexico compares to criminal violence in other settings such as mafia violence in Italy, blood feuds in Albania, and Russian contract killings in the 1990s.[32] Williams suggests that the epidemic of criminal violence in Mexico may be uniquely intense and intractable because of a "perfect storm" of conditions and different dimensions of the DTO-related violence.

The State Department maintained in its 2013 terrorism report that "there are no known international terrorist organizations operating in Mexico, and there is no evidence that any terrorist group has targeted U.S. citizens in Mexican territory." The report asserted that the Mexican government remained vigilant against domestic and international terrorist threats, and continued to disrupt and dismantle the transnational criminal organizations responsible for much of the violence in the country. The State Department's 2012 terrorism report maintained that "there was no evidence that these criminal organizations had political or ideological motivations, aside from seeking to maintain the impunity with which they conduct their criminal activities."

The 112th Congress had introduced several legislative initiatives focused on the Mexican DTOs, although none became law. For example, H.R. 1270 (McCaul), introduced in March 2011, and an updated version, H.R. 4303 (McCaul), introduced in March 2012, called for the Secretary of State to designate as foreign terrorist organizations certain Mexican drug cartels. Another proposed legislative initiative, H.R. 3401 (Mack), the Enhanced Border Security Act, ordered reported by the House Subcommittee on the Western Hemisphere, Committee on Foreign Affairs, in December 2011, would have required a counterinsurgency plan "to combat the terrorist insurgency in Mexico waged by transnational criminal organizations." (For more, see the discussion on Mexico in the "112th Congress" section below.)

Peru[33]

The brutal Shining Path (Sendero Luminoso or SL) Maoist insurgency, which the Department of State has designated as an FTO, was significantly weakened in the 1990s with the capture of its leader Abimael Guzman, who, after a new trial in 2006, was sentenced to life in prison. According to the 2013 State Department terrorism report, SL currently has a single active faction with an estimated 300 to 500 fighters, and remains "a significant threat to Peru's internal security." SL is reported to sustain itself through its involvement in drug production and trafficking and extortion of taxes from others involved in the drug trade.

---

[32] Phil Williams, "The Terrorism Debate Over Mexican Drug Trafficking Violence," *Terrorism and Political Violence*, vol. 24, no. 1 (April 2012). Phil Williams is the director of the Matthew B. Ridgway Center for International Security Studies at the University of Pittsburgh, and a former visiting research professor at the U.S. Army War College.

[33] For further background on Peru, see CRS Report R42523, *Peru: Overview of Political and Economic Conditions and Relations with the United States*, by Maureen Taft-Morales.

Until 2012, there had been two SL factions in Peru, one operating in the Apurimac, Ene, and Mantaro River Valley (VRAEM) in the south led by Victor Quispe Palomino, also known as Comrade José, and the second operating in the Upper Huallaga Valley (UHV) in the north that was led by Florindo Eleuterio Flores Hala, also known as Comrade Artemio. The UHV faction essentially collapsed in the aftermath of the capture of Artemio in February 2012; he was sentenced to life in prison in June 2013.

The remaining VRAEM faction was struck a significant blow in August 2013 when Peruvian security forces killed two top SL commanders, including the brother of Comrade José, the faction's leader, in an operation against the group. The SL faction reportedly became less active in the aftermath of that operation. In 2013, the SL carried out 49 terrorist acts, down from 87 in 2012.

In April 2014, the Peruvian government took action against an alleged SL political front group known as the Movement for Amnesty and Fundamental Rights (MOVADEF) by detaining 28 of its members and charging them with terrorism, drug trafficking, and money laundering. Those detained included Alfredo Crespo, who has served as lawyer for imprisoned SL leader Guzmán, and the founder of MOVADEF, Manuel Fajardo, although in early August 2014, a Peruvian court ordered the release of eight of those being held, including Crespo and Fajardo.[34]

Venezuela[35]

U.S. officials have expressed concerns over the past several years about Venezuela's lack of cooperation on antiterrorism efforts, the involvement of senior Venezuelan government officials in supporting the drug and arms trafficking activities of the FARC, and Venezuela's relations with Iran. Since May 2006, the Secretary of State has made an annual determination that Venezuela has not been "cooperating fully with United States antiterrorism efforts" pursuant to Section 40A of the Arms Export Control Act (AECA). The most recent determination was made in May 2014. As a result, the United States imposed an arms embargo on Venezuela in 2006, which ended all U.S. commercial arms sales and retransfers to Venezuela. (Other countries currently on the Section 40A list include Cuba, Eritrea, Iran, North Korea, and Syria, not to be confused with the "state sponsors of terrorism" list under Section 6(j) of the Export Administration Act of 1979.)

In its 2013 terrorism report, the State Department maintained that "there were credible reports that Venezuela maintained a permissive environment that allowed for support of activities that benefited known terrorist groups." It further stated that individuals linked to Colombia's two guerrillas groups—the FARC and ELN—as well as Hezbollah sympathizers and supporters, were present in Venezuela. The United States also has imposed various sanctions on Venezuelan individuals and companies for supporting the FARC, Iran, and Hezbollah. (See **Table 1** for sanctions related to the FARC. For sanctions related to Iran and Hezbollah, see "U.S. Policy and Sanctions Related to Iran in Latin America" below.)

---

[34] "Humala Mops Up SL Surrogate Movadef," *Latin American Weekly Report*, April 16, 2014; John C. K. Daly, "Peru's Shining Path in Decline as Its MOVADEF Political Arms Broadens Appeal," *Terrorism Monitor*, Vol. 12,, Issue 10, May 15, 2014; and "Sala Penal Ordena la Liberación de la Cúpula del Movadef," *El Comercio* (Peru), August 5, 2014.

[35] For additional background on Venezuela, see CRS Report R43239, *Venezuela: Background and U.S. Relations*, by Mark P. Sullivan.

According to the 2013 terrorism report, the FARC used Colombia's border areas with Venezuela for incursions into Colombia, and also used Venezuelan territory for safe haven. The State Department also reiterated in the report that the Venezuelan government has taken no action against senior government officials sanctioned by the U.S. Treasury Department for directly supporting the narcotics and arms trafficking activities of the FARC. It noted, however, that Venezuela and Colombia held-level talks on border and security issues, including an announcement in August 2013 to enhance border cooperation. More recently, Colombian President Juan Manuel Santos and Venezuelan President Nicolás Maduro met in early August 2014, with talks focused on dealing with the cross border smuggling from Venezuela into Colombia. Venezuela has continued to participate as an observer in ongoing peace talks between the FARC and the Colombian government held in Havana.

Table 1. Venezuela and FARC-Related Sanctions

To date, the United States has imposed financial sanctions against seven current or former Venezuelan government and military officials for providing support to the FARC. In September 2008, the Treasury Department froze the assets of the former interior minister, Ramón Rodríguez Chacín, and two senior intelligence officials, General Henry Rangel Silva and General Hugo Carvajal (who served as Venezuela's Director of Military Intelligence between 2004 and 2011), for allegedly helping the FARC with weapons and drug trafficking. [36]

Rodríguez Chacín was elected as governor of the state of Guárico in December 2012. General Rangel was appointed by President Chávez as defense minister in January 2012, an action that raised concern among U.S. policymakers. He stepped down in October 2012, and went on to win the governorship of the Venezuelan state of Trujillo in December 2012 elections.

On July 23, 2014, Aruban authorities detained retired General Carvajal at the request of the U.S. government, but he was released on July 27 after Dutch officials ruled that Carvajal was protected by diplomatic immunity. Carvajal had been named as Venezuela's consul general to neighboring Aruba, but had not yet been confirmed by the Dutch government. U.S. officials expressed deep disappointment with the decision of the government of the Netherlands to release Carvajal, and concern about credible reports that the Venezuelan government threated Aruba and the Netherlands to gain Carvajal's release. Some press reports allege that Venezuela threatened Aruba economically and militarily. On July 24, 2014, a Miami Federal court unsealed an indictment against Carvajal, along with two other former Venezuelan officials, for conspiring with Colombian drug traffickers to export cocaine to the United States. [37]

In September 2011, the Treasury Department imposed financial sanctions on four more Venezuelan officials for acting for or on behalf of the FARC, often in direct support of its narcotics and arms trafficking activities: Amilcar Jesus Figueroa Salazar, a member of Venezuela's delegation to the Latin American Parliament; Major General Clíver Antonio Alcalá Cordones of the Venezuelan Army; Freddy Alirio Bernal Rosales, a national legislator for the United Socialist Party of Venezuela (PSUV); and Ramon Isidro Madriz Moreno, an officer of Venezuela's intelligence service. [38]

---

[36] U.S. Department of the Treasury, "Treasury Targets Venezuelan Government Officials Supporting the FARC," September 12, 2008; *Federal Register*, September 19, 2008, pp. 54453-54454.

[37] U.S. Department of State, Daily Press Briefing, July 28, 2014; Kejal Vyas and Juan Forero, "U.S. Indicts Three Top Ex-Venezuelan Officials," *Wall Street Journal*, July 25, 2014; and Kejal Vyas and Jose de Cordoba, "Aruba Says Venezuela Pressured It Militarily," *Wall Street Journal*, July 29, 2014.

[38] U.S. Department of the Treasury, "Treasury Designates Four Venezuelan Officials for Providing Arms and Security to the FARC," September 8, 2011; *Federal Register*, September 14, 2011, pp. 56875-56876.

The 2013 terrorism report also maintained that Venezuela's border security at ports of entry is vulnerable and susceptible to corruption. It noted that the Venezuelan government did not perform biographic and biometric screening at ports of entry or exit, and that there was no automated system to collect advance passenger name records on commercial flights.

With regard to Venezuela's relations with Iran, the State Department maintained in the 2013 terrorism report that "Venezuela maintained the economic, financial, and diplomatic cooperation with Iran that the late President Hugo Chávez established during his presidency," and that President Maduro publicly strengthened to strengthen ties with Iran. In a July 2012 press interview, President Obama had expressed general concern about "Iran engaging in destabilizing activity around the globe," but indicated that his "sense is that what Mr. Chávez has done over the past several years has not had a serious national security impact on us."[39] This was reiterated by the then-head of the U.S. Southern Command, General Douglas Fraser, who maintained that he did not see Venezuela as a "national security threat," and that Iran's connection with Venezuela was primarily diplomatic and economic.[40]

In the aftermath of President Hugo Chávez's death in March 2013, some observers contended that without Chávez at the helm, Venezuela's relations with Iran could eventually begin to wane, especially since the strengthening of bilateral relations in recent years was viewed by many analysts as being driven by the personal relationship between Chávez and Iranian President Mahmoud Ahmadinejad. As discussed below, a June 2013 State Department report to Congress maintained that "Iranian influence in Latin America and the Caribbean is waning." The 2013 terrorism report stated that "Iran's influence in the Western Hemisphere remained a concern," but noted that "Iran has been unable to expand its economic and political ties in Latin America" because of "strong sanctions imposed by the United States and the EU." (For more see "U.S. Policy and Sanctions Related to Iran in Latin America" below.)

Iran's Activities in Latin America

Over the past several years, there has been concern among policymakers about Iran's growing interest and activities in Latin America, centered on Iran's attempts to work with regional governments to circumvent U.N. and U.S. sanctions. Both Iran and Hezbollah, the radical Lebanon-based Islamic group, a U.S.-designated Foreign Terrorist Organization (FTO) with which Iran has strong ties, are reported to be linked to two bombings against Jewish targets in Buenos Aires, Argentina, in the early 1990s: the 1992 bombing of the Israeli Embassy that killed 30 people; and the 1994 bombing of the Argentine-Israeli Mutual Association (AMIA) that killed 85 people (see **Table 2** on the AMIA investigation.) During the presidency of Mahmoud Ahmadinejad (2005-2013), Iran worked to increase its ties with Latin American countries, and Venezuela under President Hugo Chávez (1999-2013) arguably served as Iran's gateway to the region.

There has been disagreement, however, over the extent and significance of Iran's activities in the region. Some observers maintain that former President Mahmoud Ahmadinejad trumpeted his official visits to, and relations with, the region in an attempt to show that Iran was not isolated

---

[39] "The Situation Room," Transcript, *CNN*, July 11, 2012; and Patricia Massei and Erika Bolstad, "Mitt Romney, GOP Howl Over President Barack Obama's Remark About Hugo Chávez," *Miami Herald*, July 11, 2012.

[40] Frank Bajak, "Top U.S. General: Venezuela Not a National Security Threat," *AP Newswire*, July 31, 2012.

internationally, but that most often, statements of cooperation and support and investment in the region were largely propaganda. In the aftermath of the departure of Ahmadinejad from office and the death of Chávez in 2013, many analysts contend that Iranian relations with the region have diminished. Current Iranian President Hassan Rouhani, who took office in August 2013, campaigned as a pragmatist seeking to reduce Iran's international isolation, and his government has not placed a priority on relations with those Latin American nations that Ahmadinejad had cultivated as allies. Along these lines, Iran's already limited trade with the region has been declining, and Rouhani did not attend the summit of the Group of 77 (G77) developing countries held in Bolivia in June 2014 as reportedly planned.[41] With regard to Hezbollah, some view its regional involvement in illicit activities as a means to raise money, as opposed to the organization having an ideological agenda in Latin America or pursuing one on behalf of Iran.[42]

On the other hand, some observers contend that there is enough information to view both Iran and Hezbollah as potential threats to the Western Hemisphere. They point to their alleged role in two bombings in Argentina in 1992 and 1994; the fact that the United States has imposed sanctions on various companies and individuals in the region for their support of Iran and Hezbollah; and the role of some Iranian security personnel in an alleged 2011 plot to assassinate the Saudi Ambassador in Washington, DC. In that plot, Iran allegedly sought to recruit an agent who it thought was a member of a Mexican drug trafficking organization (but was actually a Drug Enforcement Administration confidential source). Some analysts point to Hezbollah's involvement in drug trafficking and money laundering in the region and their working relations with the FARC as evidence of the group being a threat to the Western Hemisphere.[43]

In May 2013, the Argentine prosecutor in the AMIA bombing case, Alberto Nisman, issued a 500-page report alleging that Iran has been working for decades in Latin America, setting up intelligence stations in the region by utilizing embassies, cultural organizations, and even mosques as a source of recruitment. In the report, Nisman highlighted the key role of Mohsen Rabbani (one of eight Iranian officials wanted by Argentina for the AMIA bombing) as Iran's South America "coordinator for the export of revolution," working in the tri-border countries of Argentina, Brazil, and Paraguay as well as in Chile, Colombia, and Uruguay.[44] The report also highlighted the role of Guyanese national Abdul Kadir, who Nisman maintained was an intelligence agent working for Iran and a follower of Rabbani, for establishing an Iranian intelligence network in Guyana. Kadir, a former member of Guyana's parliament, is serving a life sentence in the United States for his role in a 2007 plot to bomb a jet fuel artery at John F. Kennedy International Airport in New York. The Nisman report contended that the 1994 AMIA bombing was not an isolated act, but was part of a regional strategy involving Iran's establishment of intelligence bases in several countries utilizing political, religious, and cultural

---

[41] Amelie Meyer-Robinson, "Iran-South America Trade Suffers as Relations Thaw with the West," *Global Risk Insights*, June 26, 2014.

[42] For example, see Steven Dudley, Co-Director, Insight Crime, "Terrorism and Crime in the Americas—'It's Business,'" Remarks before the Inter-American Committee Against Terrorism, Organization of American States, February 26, 2014, at: http://www.oas.org/en/sms/cicte/Documents/Sessions/2014/CICTE%20INF%208%20REMARKS%20BY%20MR%20STEVEN%20DUDLEY%20CICTE00902E04.pdf

[43] See Testimony of Douglas Farah, President, IBC Consultants LLC, before the House Financial Services Committee, Subcommittee on Monetary Policy and Trade, Hearing on "A Legislative Proposal Entitled the 'Bank Account Seizure of Terrorist Assets (BASTA) Act,'" July 17, 2014, at: http://financialservices.house.gov/uploadedfiles/hhrg-113-ba19-wstate-dfarah-20140717.pdf

[44] Alberto Nisman, Fiscal General, Ministerio Público de la Nación, Argentina, Dictamina, May 29, 2013.

institutions that could be used to support terrorist acts. On the other hand, most of the activities discussed in the Nisman report were carried out years ago and are not necessarily representative of Iran's current approach toward Latin America.

No matter the scope of Iran's involvement in the region, it is important to remember that Iran's key foreign policy focus remains its immediate region. It is in the Middle East, and South and Central Asia, where the Iranian regime perceives potential threats to its survival, and in which Iran has, for ideological, religious, and political motives, tried to alter political outcomes in its favor. Whatever efforts Iran has made to engage like-minded leaders in Latin America, these efforts do not approach its level of involvement in countries such as Iraq, Afghanistan, Syria, or Lebanon.[45]

Table 2. AMIA Bombing Investigation

Argentine Special Prosecutor Alberto Nisman was appointed to lead the AMIA investigation in 2004. Until then, progress on the investigation and prosecution of those responsible for the 1994 bombing had been stymied because of the government's mishandling of the case. In September 2004, a three-judge panel acquitted all 22 Argentine defendants in the case and faulted the shortcomings of the original investigation. With Nisman's appointment in 2004, however, the government moved forward with a new investigation. As a result, an Argentine judge issued arrest warrants in November 2006 for nine foreign individuals: an internationally wanted Hezbollah militant from Lebanon, Imad Mughniyah (subsequently killed by a car bomb in Damascus Syria in 2008), and eight Iranian government officials. INTERPOL, the International Criminal Police Organization, subsequently posted Red Notices (international wanted persons notices) in 2007 for Mughniyah and five of the Iranian officials: Ali Fallahijan, Mohsen Rabbani, Ahmad Reza Asghari, Ahmad Vahidi (Iran's current defense minister), and Mohsen Rezai.[46] In 2009, Argentina also issued an arrest warrant for the capture of Samuel Salman El Reda, a Colombian citizen thought to be living in Lebanon, alleged to have coordinated a Hezbollah cell that carried out the bombing; he was subsequently added to the INTERPOL Red Notice list.

The State Department's 2011 terrorism report maintained that Argentina continued its efforts to bring to justice those suspected in the AMIA bombing, but noted that the government had shifted its stance with respect to engagement with Iran over the issue. In 2011, President Cristina Fernández de Kirchner indicated Argentina's willingness to enter into a dialogue with the Iranian government despite its refusal to turn over suspects in the case. Several rounds of talks with Iran were held in 2012, with Argentine Foreign Minister Hector Timerman leading the effort.

In January 2013, Argentina announced that it had reached an agreement with Iran, and signed a memorandum of understanding, to establish a joint Truth Commission made up of impartial jurists from third countries to review the bombing case. After extensive debate, Argentina's Congress completed its approval of the agreement on February 28, 2013. Argentina's two main Jewish groups, AMIA and the Delegation of Israeli Associations (DAIA), strongly opposed the agreement because they believe that it could guarantee impunity for the Iranian suspects.[47] Several U.S. Members of Congress also expressed their strong concerns about the Truth Commission because they believed it could jeopardize Argentina's AMIA investigation

---

[45] For additional background on Iran and its foreign policy, see CRS Report RL32048, *Iran: U.S. Concerns and Policy Responses*, by Kenneth Katzman.

[46] INTERPOL, Media Release, "INTERPOL General Assembly Upholds Executive Committee Decision on AMIA Red Notice Dispute," November 7, 2007. The three other Iranians wanted by Argentina not included on INTERPOL's red notice list are former President Ali Akbar Hashemi-Rafsanjani; former Foreign Minister Ali Akbar Velayati; former Iranian Ambassador to Argentina Hadi Soleimanpour.

[47] "A Perverse Manoeuvre in Argentina," *Latin News Daily*, February 28, 2013.

> and charges against the Iranians.
>
> In May 2014, an Argentine court declared unconstitutional the agreement with Iran to jointly investigate the AMIA bombing. Special Prosecutor Nisman had maintained that the agreement with Iran constituted an "undue interference of the executive branch in the exclusive sphere of the judiciary." [48] The Fernández government maintained that it would appeal the ruling to Argentina's Supreme Court.

Background on Iran in Latin America

Iran's ties to the region predate its recent increased attention. Venezuela's relations with Iran have been long-standing because they were both founding members of OPEC in 1960. In the aftermath of the 1979 Iranian revolution, Iran fostered closer relations with Cuba and with Nicaragua (after the 1979 Sandinista revolution). Under the government of President Mohammed Khatami (1997-2005), Iran made efforts to increase its trade with Latin America, particularly Brazil, and there were also efforts to increase cooperation with Venezuela. Venezuelan President Hugo Chávez visited Iran in 2001 and 2003, which led to a joint venture agreement to produce tractors in Venezuela.[49]

Not until President Ahmadinejad's rule began in 2005, however, did Iran aggressively work to increase its diplomatic and economic linkages with Latin American countries. A major rationale for this increased focus on Latin America was Iran's efforts to overcome its international isolation and reduce the effect of increasing sanctions. The personal relationship between Ahmadinejad and Venezuelan President Hugo Chávez also drove the strengthening of bilateral ties. The two nations signed a variety of agreements in agriculture, petrochemicals, oil exploration in the Orinoco region of Venezuela, the manufacturing of automobiles, and housing. Weekly flights between the two countries began in 2007, but were curtailed in September 2010.[50] The State Department had expressed concern about these flights, maintaining that they were only subject to cursory immigration and customs controls.

Venezuela under Hugo Chávez also played a key role in the development of Iran's expanding relations with other countries in the region. This outreach largely focused on leftist governments that share the goal of reducing U.S. influence in the region. In recent years, Iran's relations have grown with Bolivia under President Evo Morales, with Ecuador under President Rafael Correa, and with Nicaragua under President Daniel Ortega. While Iran has promised assistance and investment to these countries, observers maintain that there is little evidence that such promises have been fulfilled.[51]

---

[48] "Argentine Court Declares Bombing Probe with Iran Unconstitutional," *Agence France Presse*, May 16, 2014.

[49] Farideh Farhi "Tehran's Perspective on Iran-Latin American Relations," in *Iran in Latin America: Threat or 'Axis of Annoyance'?*, Woodrow Wilson International Center for Scholars, 2009 (based on July 2008 conference), edited by Cynthia Arnson, Haleh Esfandiari, and Adam Stubits, available at http://www.wilsoncenter.org/sites/default/files/Iran_in_LA.pdf.

[50] "House Foreign Affairs, Subcommittee on Middle East and South Asia, and Subcommittee on Western Hemisphere, and House Oversight and Government Reform, Subcommittee on National Security, Homeland Defense and Foreign Operations Hold Joint Hearing on Venezuela's Sanctionable Activity," *CQ Congressional Transcripts*, June 24, 2011; and "House Foreign Affairs Committee Holds Hearing on Threats and Security in the Western Hemisphere," *CQ Congressional Transcripts*, October 13, 2011.

[51] For example, see Kavon "Hak" Hakimzadeh, "Iran & Venezuela: The Axis of Annoyance," *Military Review*, May 1, 2009; and Anne-Marie O'Connor and Mary Beth Sheridan, "Iran's Invisible Nicaragua Embassy: Feared Stronghold (continued...)

From 2006-2013, Iranian President Ahmadinejad visited Latin America eight times, most often Venezuela, but also visited Bolivia, Brazil, Ecuador, Nicaragua, and Cuba. In 2012, Ahmadinejad undertook two trips to the region: a visit in January to Cuba, Ecuador, Nicaragua, and Venezuela; and a June trip to Brazil to attend the U.N. Conference on Sustainable Development in Rio de Janeiro (which notably did not include bilateral meetings with the Brazilian government) along with side trips to Bolivia and Venezuela. In 2013, Ahmadinejad attended the funeral for President Chávez, who died in early March 2013 after battling cancer.

While Ahmadinejad's January 2012 trip to Venezuela, Nicaragua, Cuba, and Ecuador increased concerns of some U.S. policymakers about Iran's efforts to deepen ties with Latin America, some policy analysts and U.S. officials contend that the trip was not successful. Analysts point out that leaders' statements during these trips are largely propaganda, with the official Iranian press trumpeting relations with these countries in order to show that Iran is not isolated internationally and that it has good relations with countries geographically close to the United States.[52] The January 2012 trip was restricted to meeting with four leftist governments that have often opposed U.S. policy in the region and have limited regional influence. The fact that the tour notably did not include a trip to Brazil to meet with President Dilma Rousseff detracted from the significance of the visit to the region. A close adviser to Ahmadinejad maintained in an interview in the Brazilian press that President Rousseff had "destroyed years of good relations" between Iran and Brazil.[53] Director of National Intelligence James Clapper testified before Congress in late January 2012 that while the U.S. intelligence community remained concerned about Iran's connection with Venezuela, Ahmadinejad's trip to Latin America "was not all that successful."[54]

On the diplomatic front, Iran under President Ahmadinejad opened six embassies in Latin America by 2009—Bolivia, Chile, Colombia, Ecuador, Nicaragua and Uruguay. This was in addition to existing embassies in Argentina, Brazil, Cuba, Mexico, and Venezuela.[55] Iran also reportedly has 36 Shi'a cultural centers in 17 countries throughout the region, according to March 2012 congressional testimony of then-SOUTHCOM Commander Douglas Fraser.[56] In January 2012, Iran also launched a Spanish-language satellite TV network as part of its ideological battle to counter what it views as biased reporting—then-President Ahmadinejad said that it would help end the West's "hegemony" of the airwaves.[57] Reports that Iran was building a large embassy in

---

(...continued)

Never Materialized," *Washington Post*, July 13, 2009. Also see "House Foreign Affairs Committee Holds Hearing on Democracy in Nicaragua," *CQ Congressional Transcripts*, December 1, 2011.

[52] Comments by Stephen Johnson, Center for Strategic and International Studies, and Afshin Molavi, New America Foundation, at a January 19, 2012, event sponsored by the Council of the Americas (Washington, DC) on "Iran in the Americas: A Readout of the Visit."

[53] Simon Romero, "Iranian Adviser Accuses Brazil of Ruining Relations," *New York Times*, January 24, 2012. Subsequently, the Iranian adviser denied part of the interview, and stressed that relations between Iran and Brazil are good, see "Iranian Aide Says Foreign Media Distorted His Interview on Ties with Brazil," *BBC Monitoring Newsfile* (text of report by Iranian official government news agency IRNA) January 24, 2012.

[54] "Senate Select Intelligence Committee Holds Hearing on Worldwide Threats," *CQ Congressional Transcripts*, January 31, 2012.

[55] Anne-Marie O'Connor and Mary Beth Sheridan, "Iran's Invisible Nicaragua Embassy; Feared Stronghold Never Materialized," *Washington Post*, July 13, 2009.

[56] U.S. Congress, Senate Committee on Armed Services, *Oversight: U.S. Southern Command and U.S. Northern Command*, Hearing, 112th Cong., 2nd sess., March 13, 2012.

[57] Jim Wyss, "Iran's HispanTV Aims to Woo Latino Viewers," *Miami Herald*, January 31, 2012.

Managua, Nicaragua turned out to be erroneous.[58] Other reports that Iran's embassy in Venezuela is one of the largest in the world were also inaccurate. State Department officials maintain that there are many embassies in Caracas that have a diplomatic presence far larger than that of Iran, including the U.S. Embassy.[59]

An April 2010 unclassified Department of Defense report to Congress on Iran's military power (required by Section 1245 of the National Defense Authorization Act for FY2010, P.L. 111-84) maintained that Iran's Qods Force, which maintains operational capabilities around the world, had increased its presence in Latin America in recent years, particularly in Venezuela.[60] At the same time, however, then-commander of the U.S. Southern Command, General Douglas Fraser, maintained that the focus of Iran in the region was diplomatic and commercial, and that he had not seen an increase in Iran's military presence in the region.[61] In July 2012, General Fraser maintained in a press interview that Iran's relationship with Venezuela was primarily diplomatic and economic and that Iran's ties with Venezuela did not amount to a military alliance.[62]

In December 2011, a documentary featured on the Spanish-language network *Univisión* alleged that Iranian and Venezuelan diplomats in Mexico tried to recruit Mexican students for plotting possible cyber attacks against the United States. There is no indication that U.S. officials have been able to corroborate the allegations in the documentary. However, the State Department subsequently declared persona non grata the Venezuelan Consul General in Miami, Livia Acosta, who had been based in Mexico at the time of the documentary.

As noted above, another reason for U.S. concerns about Iran's deepening relations with Latin America is its ties to Hezbollah, which along with Iran, is reported to have been linked to two bombings against Jewish targets in Argentina in the early 1990s. In recent years, U.S. concerns regarding Hezbollah in Latin America have focused on its fundraising activities among sympathizers in the region, particularly the tri-border area (TBA) of Argentina, Brazil, and Paraguay (see **Figure 2**), but also in other parts of the region.[63] At the same time, U.S. officials point out that Hezbollah's primary funding is from Iran, and not from fundraising activities in Latin America. The Brazilian city of Foz do Iguaçu and the Paraguayan city of Ciudad del Este have large Muslim populations. The TBA has long been used for arms and drug trafficking, contraband smuggling, document and currency fraud, money laundering, and the manufacture and movement of pirated goods.

---

[58] Ibid.; and Sylvie Lanteaume, "Iran's Hand in Latin America Not as U.S. Feared," *Agence France Presse*, July 14, 2009.

[59] "House Foreign Affairs, Subcommittee on Middle East and South Asia, and Subcommittee on Western Hemisphere, and House Oversight and Government Reform, Subcommittee on National Security, Homeland Defense and Foreign Operations Hold Joint Hearing on Venezuela's Sanctionable Activity," *CQ Congressional Transcripts*, June 24, 2011.

[60] Department of Defense, "Unclassified Report on Military Power of Iran," April 2010. For the full text of the report, see http://www.politico.com/static/PPM145_link_042010 html. For background on the Qods Force, see CRS Report RL32048, *Iran: U.S. Concerns and Policy Responses*, by Kenneth Katzman.

[61] Anne Flaherty, *"Pentagon Says Iran's Reach in Latin America Doesn't Pose Military Threat,"* AP Newswire, April 27, 2010. General Fraser reiterated that Iran's focus in Latin America has been "primarily diplomatic and commercial," in March 30, 2011, testimony before the House Armed Services Committee. See "Hearing of the House Armed Services Committee; Subject FY2012 National Defense Authorization Budget Requests for the U.S. Southern Command, U.S. Northern Command, and U.S. European Command," *Federal News Service*, March 30, 2011.

[62] Frank Bajak, "Top U.S. General: Venezuela Not a National Security Threat," *Associated Press*, July 31, 2012.

[63] For additional background, see *Threat Convergence in South America's Tri-Border Area (TBA)*, The Fund for Peace, Center for the Study of Threat Convergence, Factsheet Series, January 11, 2010; and Rensselaer Lee, "Dispatches: The Tri-Border-Terrorism Nexus," *Global Crime*, Vol. 9, No 4, November 2008.

Figure 2. Tri-Border Area of Argentina, Brazil, and Paraguay

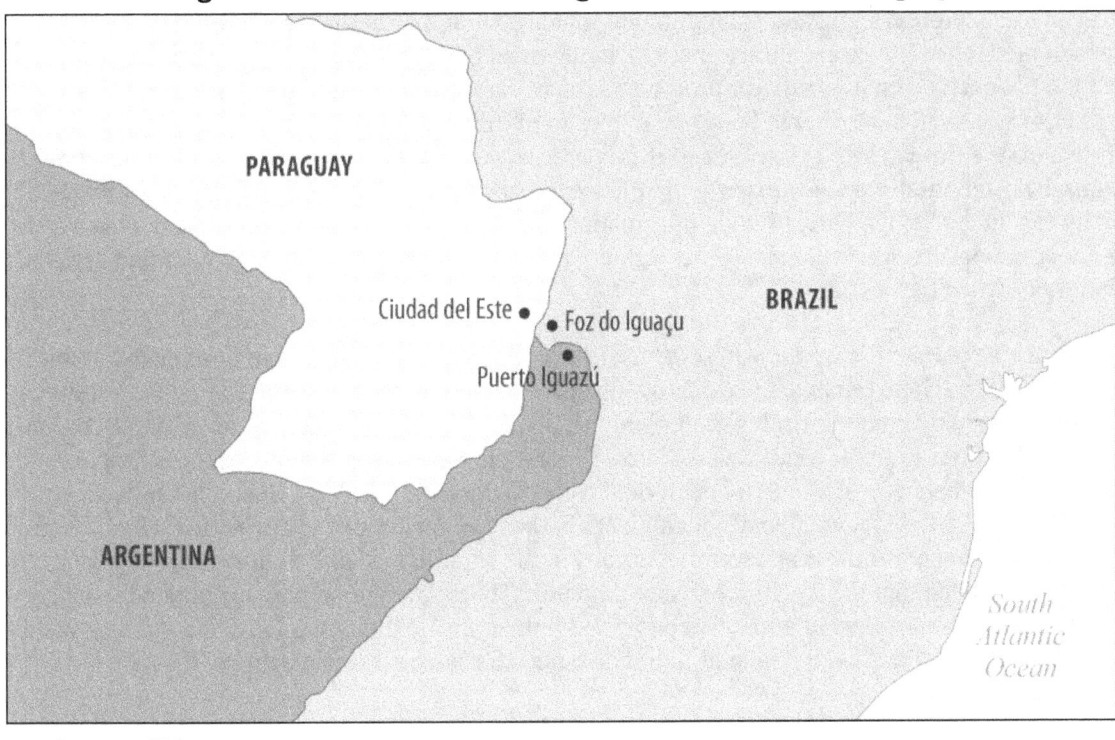

Source: CRS.

U.S. Policy and Sanctions Related to Iran in Latin America

Since 2011, Congress has focused extensively on concerns regarding the activities of both Iran and Hezbollah in the region. Several House and Senate Committee hearings have been held, and most significantly, in December 2012, Congress enacted the Countering Iran in the Western Hemisphere Act of 2012 (P.L. 112-220). As enacted, the measure required the Secretary of State to conduct an assessment within 180 days of the "threats posed to the United States by Iran's growing presence and activity in the Western Hemisphere" and to develop a strategy to address these threats.

Submitted to Congress in late June 2013, the State Department report was mostly classified, but as specified in the law, also included an unclassified summary of policy recommendations.[64] The State Department maintained in the unclassified portion of the report that "Iranian influence in Latin America and the Caribbean is waning" because of U.S. diplomatic outreach, the strengthening of allies' capacity to disrupt illicit Iranian activity, international nonproliferation efforts, a strong sanctions policy, and Iran's poor management of its foreign relations. The report also stated that current U.S., European Union, and U.N. Security Council sanctions have limited the economic relationship between the region and Iran.

The State Department report outlined four lines of action that the U.S. government is undertaking to decrease Iran's presence and influence in the region: **border security and enforcement**, in

---

[64] U.S. Department of State, "Annex A, Unclassified Summary of Policy Recommendations," included in report to Congress required by the Countering Iran in the Western Hemisphere Act of 2012 (P.L. 112-220), June 2013.

which the United States works closely with nations in the hemisphere to detect and disrupt illicit travel, trade, proliferation, and smuggling by Iran and its surrogates or proxies; **diplomacy**, in which the United States encourages nations in the hemisphere to join efforts to persuade Iran to address concerns about its nuclear program, support for terrorism, and human rights abuses; **sanctions**, in which the United States continues to monitor closely all sanctionable activity by Iran and its surrogates and proxies, and is prepared to take appropriate action to address such activities; and **intelligence sharing** with allies and partners to collect information on Iranian activities in the hemisphere, provide information about malign Iranian activities, and work with partner nations to ensure they have the capacity to detect and address subversive Iranian actions before or when they occur.

The State Department's *Country Reports on Terrorism 2013* stated that "Iran's influence in the Western Hemisphere remained a concern," but also noted that "due to strong sanctions imposed on the country by both the United States and the EU, Iran has been unable to expand its economic and political ties in Latin America." As in past years, the State Department's terrorism report also asserted that there are "no known operational cells of either Al Qaeda or Hezbollah in the hemisphere," but that ideological sympathizers in the region continue to "provide financial and ideological support to these and terrorist groups in the Middle East and South Asia." The 2013 report also stated that the tri-border area of Argentina, Brazil, and Paraguay "continued to be an important regional nexus of arms, narcotics, and human trafficking; counterfeiting; pirated goods; and money laundering—all potential funding sources for terrorist organizations."[65]

In presenting the 2014 posture statement of the U.S. Southern Command (SOUTHCOM) to Congress, General John Kelly asserted that the exact amount of profits generated by these illicit activities is unclear, but it is likely to be "at least…in the tens of millions of dollars." With regard to Hezbollah, General Kelly stated that he remains "concerned that the group maintains an operational presence there." He stated that "members, supporters and adherents of Islamic extremist groups are present in Latin America," and proffered that "Islamic extremists visit the region to proselytize, recruit, establish business venues to generate funds, and expand their radical networks." According to Kelly, "some Muslim communities in the Caribbean and South America are exhibiting increasingly extremist ideology and activities, mostly as a result from ideologues' activities and external influence from the Middle East, Africa, and South Asia." Kelly also maintained that "as a state sponsor of terrorism, Iran's involvement in the Western Hemisphere is a matter for concern."[66] In his March 2013 congressional testimony on SOUTHCOM's 2013 posture statement, General Kelly had stated that "Iran is struggling to maintain influence in the region," and that "its efforts to cooperate with a small set of countries with interests that are inimical to the United States are waning." According to General Kelly, while "the Iranian regime has increased its diplomatic and economic outreach across the region with nations like Venezuela, Bolivia, Ecuador, and Argentina," the "outreach has only been marginally successful ... and the region as a whole has not been receptive to Iranian efforts."[67]

---

[65] U.S. Department of State, *Country Reports on Terrorism 2013*, April 2014.

[66] Posture Statement of General John F. Kelly, Commander, U.S. Southern Command, before the 113th Congress, House Armed Services Committee, February 26, 2014, available at: http://www.southcom.mil/newsroom/Documents/2014_SOUTHCOM_Posture_Statement_HASC_FINAL_PDF.pdf

[67] General John F. Kelly, Commander, United States Southern Command, Posture Statement, Senate Armed Services Committee, March 19, 2013, available at http://www.armed-services.senate.gov/statemnt/2013/03%20March/Kelly%2003-19-13.pdf.

In October 2011, the Department of Justice filed criminal charges against a dual Iranian-American citizen from Texas, Manssor Arbabsiar, and a member of Iran's Qods Force in Iran, Gholam Shakuri, for their alleged participation in a bizarre plot to kill the Saudi Ambassador in Washington, DC. The indictment alleged that Arbabsiar met several times in Mexico City with an informant of the U.S. Drug Enforcement Administration (DEA) posing as a member of one of Mexico's most violent drug trafficking organization, Los Zetas, and had arranged to hire the informant to murder the Ambassador with the financial support of Shakuri.[68] Arbabsiar subsequently pled guilty and was sentenced in May 2013 to 25 years in prison.[69]

At the time, U.S. officials expressed concern about the implications of the failed Iranian plot on the nexus between terrorist and criminal groups as well as on Iran's intentions. The DEA testified in November 2011 that the alleged plot "illustrates the extent to which terrorist organizations will align themselves with other criminals to achieve their goals."[70] Director of National Intelligence (DNI) James Clapper stated before the Senate Select Committee on Intelligence in January 2012 that the plot to kill the Saudi Ambassador shows that "some Iranian officials ... are now more willing to conduct an attack in the United States," and he expressed concern "about Iranian plotting against U.S. or allied interests overseas."[71] In March 2013, DNI Clapper again testified before the Senate Select Committee on Intelligence that the failed 2011 plot against the Saudi Ambassador in Washington showed that Iran may be willing to attack in the United States in response to perceived offenses against the regime.[72]

To date, the United States has imposed sanctions against several Venezuelan companies because of their connections to Iran.

- In 2008, the State Department imposed sanctions on the Venezuelan Military Industries Company (CAVIM) pursuant to the Iran, North Korea, and Syria Nonproliferation Act (P.L. 109-353) for allegedly violating a ban on technology that could assist Iran in the development of weapons systems.[73] The sanctions prohibited any U.S. government procurement or assistance to the company. While these sanctions expired in 2010, they were imposed once again in May 2011 for a two-year period, and again in February 2013 for a two-year period.[74]

---

[68] U.S. Department of Justice, "Two Men Charged in Alleged Plot to Assassinate Saudi Arabian Ambassador to the United States," Press Release, October 11, 2011, available at http://www.justice.gov/opa/pr/2011/October/11-ag-1339.html.

[69] U.S. Department of Justice, The United States Attorney's Office, Southern District of New York, "Manssor Arbabsiar Sentenced In Manhattan Federal Court to 25 years in Prison for Conspiring with Iranian Military Officials to Assassinate the Saudi Arabian Ambassador to the United States," May 30, 2013.

[70] U.S. Congress, House Committee on Foreign Affairs, Subcommittee on Terrorism, Nonproliferation, and Trade, *Counterterrorism and the Con Re o Enforcement rt*, 112th Cong., 1st sess., November 17, 2011, Serial No. 112-81 (Washington: GPO, 2011), written testimony of Derek S. Maltz, Special Agent in charge of the Special Operations Division, Drug Enforcement Administration, available at http://foreignaffairs.house.gov/112/mal111711.pdf.

[71] Testimony of Director of National Intelligence James Clapper, January 31, 2012, op. cit.

[72] James R. Clapper, Director of National Intelligence, "Worldwide Threat Assessment of the US Intelligence Community," Statement for the Record, Senate Select Committee on Intelligence, March 12, 2013, available at http://intelligence.senate.gov/130312/clapper.pdf.

[73] Although the sanction became effective in August 2008, it was not published in the *Federal Register* until October 2008. See *Federal Register*, pp. 63226-63227, October 23, 2008.

[74] Department of State, "Bureau of International Security and Nonproliferation Imposition of Nonproliferation (continued...)

- In 2008, the U.S. Treasury Department imposed sanctions on an Iranian-owned bank based in Caracas, the Banco Internacional de Desarollo, C.A., under Executive Order 13382 that allows the President to block the assets of proliferators of weapons of mass destruction and their supporters. The bank is linked to the Export Development Bank of Iran (EDBI), which the Treasury Department asserts has provided or attempted to provide services to Iran's Ministry of Defense and Armed Forces Logistics.[75]

- In May 2011, the United States imposed sanctions on Venezuela's state oil company, Petróleos de Venezuela S.A. (PdVSA), pursuant to the Comprehensive Iran Sanctions, Accountability, and Disinvestment Act of 2010 (P.L. 111-195), because the company provided $50 million worth of reformate, an additive used in gasoline, to Iran between December 2010 and March 2011. Specifically, the State Department imposed three sanctions on PdVSA to prohibit it from competing for U.S. government procurement contracts, securing financing from the Export-Import Bank, and obtaining U.S. export licenses. The sanctions specifically exclude PdVSA subsidiaries (Citgo) and do not prohibit the export of oil to the United States.[76]

The United States has also imposed sanctions on individuals and companies in Latin America for providing support to Hezbollah. At times, sanctions have been connected to law enforcement cases, including cases involving the U.S. Drug Enforcement Administration.

- Since 2006, the Treasury Department has sanctioned over a dozen individuals and several entities in the TBA for providing financial support to Hezbollah leadership in Lebanon.[77]

- In June 2008, the Treasury Department imposed sanctions (pursuant to Executive Order 13224 as Specially Designated Global Terrorists) on two Venezuelans— Ghazi Nasr al Din (a Venezuelan diplomat serving in Lebanon) and Fawzi Kan'an—for providing financial and other support to Hezbollah. U.S. citizens are prohibited from engaging in any transactions with the two Venezuelans, including any business with two travel agencies in Caracas owned by Kan'an.[78]

- In October 2008, U.S. and Colombian investigators dismantled a cocaine trafficking and money laundering ring that reportedly used part of its profits to finance Hezbollah.[79]

(...continued)

Measures Against Foreign Persons, Including a Ban on U.S. Government Procurement," 78 █e█er█Re█ister 9768-9769, February 11, 2013.

[75] U.S. Department of the Treasury, Press Release, "Export Development Bank of Iran Designated as a Proliferator," October 22, 2008.

[76] U.S. Department of State, "Seven Companies Sanctioned Under the Amended Iran Sanctions Act," Fact Sheet, May 24, 2011.

[77] U.S. Congress, House Committee on Foreign Affairs, █mer█in█T█re█ts █n██e█urity in t█e █estern █emisp█ere█ █e██teps █or ████o█i█y, 112th Cong., 1st sess., October 13, 2011, Serial No. 112-75 (Washington: GPO, 2011), written testimony of U.S. Department of the Treasury's Assistant Secretary for Terrorist Financing Daniel L. Glaser available at http://foreignaffairs.house.gov/112/gla101311.pdf.

[78] "Treasury Targets Hizballah in Venezuela," █t█tes █e█s █er█i█e, June 18, 2008.

[79] "Colombia Ties Drug Ring to Hezbollah," █e█ █or█Times, October 22, 2008.

- In December 2010, the Treasury Department sanctioned Hezbollah's chief representative in South America, Bilal Mohsen Wehbe, for transferring funds collected in Brazil to Lebanon. He also reportedly had been responsible for overseeing Hezbollah's counterintelligence activities in the TBA.[80]

- In February 2011, the Treasury Department identified the Lebanon-based Lebanese Canadian Bank (LCB) for its role in facilitating the money laundering activities of an international narcotics trafficking and money laundering network with ties to Hezbollah, and imposed sanctions that effectively prohibited the bank from operating in the United States. The Treasury Department maintained that the network was involved in moving illegal drugs from South America to Europe and the Middle East via West Africa.[81]

- Following on from the U.S. investigation of the LCB, in November 2011, the Department of Justice announced the federal criminal indictment of Lebanese citizen Ayman Joumaa (who had been designated by the Treasury Department as a narcotics trafficker and money launder in January 2011) for conspiring to coordinate shipments of cocaine from Colombia through Central America for sale to Los Zetas, one of Mexico's most violent drug trafficking organizations. The indictment alleged that Joumaa laundered hundreds of millions of dollars in drug trafficking proceeds from Europe, Mexico, the United States, and West Africa for cocaine suppliers in Colombia and Venezuela.[82] A civil indictment filed by the Department of Justice in December 2011 alleged that Joumaa's drug trafficking organization operates in Lebanon, West Africa, Panama, and Colombia, and launders proceeds from illicit activities through various channels, including bulk cash smuggling operations and Lebanese exchange houses, and pays fees to Hezbollah to facilitate the transportation and laundering of the proceeds.[83]

- In June 2012, the Treasury Department designated four additional individuals (including three dual Lebanese-Venezuelan citizens) and three companies (two in Colombia and one in Venezuela) involved in Ayman Joumaa's drug money laundering network. At the same time, a Lebanese Colombian national, Ali Mohamad Saleh, was also designated as a Specially Designated Global Terrorist pursuant to Executive Order 13224 for directing and coordinating Hezbollah activity in Colombia.[84]

- In July 2013, the Treasury Department designated two Colombian nationals as well as 29 other individuals and entities, including companies located in

---

[80] "Treasury Targets Hizballah Financial Network," ☐ep☐rtment o☐t☐e Tre☐sury ☐o☐uments, Press Release, December 9, 2010.

[81] U.S. Department of the Treasury, "Treasury Identifies Lebanese Canadian Bank Sal as a Primary Money Laundering Concern," Press Release, February 10, 2011.

[82] U.S. Department of Justice, U.S. Attorney's Office—Eastern District of Virginia, "U.S. Charges Alleged Lebanese Drug Kingpin with Laundering Drug Proceeds for Mexican and Colombian Drug Cartels," Press Release, December 13, 2011; Jo Becker, "Beirut Bank Seen as a Hub of Hezbollah's Financing," ☐e☐ ☐or☐Times, December 14, 2011.

[83] U.S. Drug Enforcement Administration, "DEA News: Civil Suit Exposes Lebanese Money Laundering Scheme for Hizballah," News Release, December 15, 2011, available at http://www.justice.gov/dea/pubs/pressrel/pr121511 html.

[84] U.S. Department of the Treasury, "Treasury Targets Major Money Laundering Network Linked to Drug Trafficker Ayman Joumaa and a Key Hizballah Supporter in South America," Press Release, June 27, 2012, available at http://www.treasury.gov/press-center/press-releases/Pages/tg1624.aspx; Abraham Mahshie, "Hezbollah Financing Evolves Beyond Colombia's Muslim Communities," ☐i☐mi ☐er☐☐, December 19, 2013.

Colombia, Panama, and Israel as Specially Designated Narcotics Traffickers involved in a money laundering network connected to drug trafficking organizations, including one run by Ayman Joumaa noted above that has benefited Hezbollah.[85]

U.S. Policy

As in other parts of the world, the United States has assisted Latin American and Caribbean nations over the years in their struggle against terrorist or insurgent groups indigenous to the region. For example, in the 1980s, the United States supported the government of El Salvador with significant economic and military assistance in its struggle against a leftist guerrilla insurgency. In recent years, the United States has employed various policy tools to combat terrorism in the Latin America and Caribbean region, including sanctions, anti-terrorism assistance and training, law enforcement cooperation, and multilateral cooperation through the OAS. Moreover, given the nexus between terrorism and drug trafficking, one can argue that assistance and sanctions aimed at combating drug trafficking organizations in the Andean region have also been a means of combating terrorism by cutting off a source of revenue for terrorist organizations. The same argument can be made regarding efforts to combat money laundering in the region.[86]

Although terrorism was not the main focus of U.S. policy toward the region in recent years, attention increased in the aftermath of the 9/11 terrorist attacks on New York and Washington. Anti-terrorism assistance has increased along with bilateral and regional cooperation against terrorism. Congress approved the Bush Administration's request in 2002 to expand the scope of U.S. assistance to Colombia beyond a counternarcotics focus to include counterterrorism assistance to the government in its military efforts against drug-financed leftist guerrillas and rightist paramilitaries. Border security with Mexico also became a prominent issue in bilateral relations, with attention focused on the potential transit of terrorists through Mexico to the United States.

U.S. Sanctions

The United States has imposed sanctions on three groups in Colombia (ELN, FARC, and AUC) and one group in Peru (SL) designated by the Department of State as FTOs. Official designation of such groups as FTOs triggers a number of sanctions, including visa restrictions and the blocking of any funds of these groups in U.S. financial institutions. The designation also has the effect of increasing public awareness about these terrorist organizations and the concerns that the United States has about them. Numerous groups, individuals, and companies in the region with links to the above and other terrorist groups (such as Hezbollah) have also been sanctioned by the Treasury Department for drug trafficking under the Foreign Narcotics Kingpin Designation Act, Executive Order 13224 (Blocking Property and Prohibiting Transactions with Persons Who Commit, Threaten to Commit, or Support Terrorism), and Executive Order 12978 (Blocking

---

[85] U.S. Department of the Treasury, "Treasury Targets Major Money Laundering Network Operating Out of Colombia," Press Release, July 9, 2013, available at http://www.treasury.gov/press-center/press-releases/Pages/jl2002.aspx

[86] For background on interaction between criminal organizations and terrorist groups, see CRS Report R41004, *Terrorism □n□Tr□nsn□tion□□Crime□□orei□n □o□□y □ssues □or Con□ress*, by John W. Rollins and Liana Rosen.

Assets and Prohibiting Transactions with Significant Narcotics Traffickers). As noted above, the United States has included Cuba on its list of state sponsors of terrorism since 1982, pursuant to Section 6(j) of the EAA, and both Cuba and Venezuela are currently on the annual Section 40A AECA list of countries that are not cooperating fully with U.S. antiterrorism efforts, lists that trigger a number of sanctions.

As described above, the United States has also imposed financial sanctions on several Venezuelan government and military officials for supporting the FARC's weapons and drug trafficking, and has imposed sanctions on three Venezuelan companies for their support of Iran. With regard to Hezbollah, the United States has imposed sanctions on individuals and companies in the region—including in Colombia and Venezuela and in the TBA of South America—for providing financial support to the organization. The Department of Justice has also pursued cases against entities and individuals involving a drug money laundering network in the region with ties to Hezbollah.

U.S. Assistance and Other Support

The United States provides assistance to improve Latin American countries' counterterrorism capabilities through several types of programs administered by the Department of State, including an Anti-Terrorism Assistance (ATA) program and an Export Control and Related Border Security (EXBS) program. The programs are funded through the Nonproliferation, Anti-terrorism, Demining, and Related Programs (NADR) foreign aid funding account.

The largest of these is the ATA program, which over the years has provided training and equipment to Latin American countries to help improve their capabilities in such areas as airport security management, hostage negotiations, bomb detection and deactivation, and countering terrorism financing. Such training was expanded to Argentina in the aftermath of the two bombings in 1992 and 1994. Assistance was also stepped up in 1997 to Argentina, Brazil, and Paraguay in light of increased U.S. concern over illicit activities in the tri-border area of those countries. In recent years, ATA for Western Hemisphere countries amounted to $7.3 million in FY2013 and an estimated $8 million in FY2014. For FY2015, the Administration requested $5.1 million in ATA for Western Hemisphere countries, with $1.75 million for Mexico, $0.8 million for Colombia, and $2.5 million for other Latin American countries through a regional program.

The EXBS program helps countries develop export and border control systems in order to prevent states and terrorist organizations from acquiring weapons of mass destruction, their delivery systems, and destabilizing conventional weapons. Latin American countries received $2.89 million in EXBS funding in FY2013 and an estimated $3 million in FY2014. The Administration requested $3 million for FY2015, with assisted slated for Argentina, Brazil, Chile, Mexico, Panama, Peru, and a regional program.

A number of Latin American countries participate in U.S.-government port security programs administered by the Department of Homeland Security (DHS) and the Department of Energy. The Container Security Initiative (CSI) operated by the U.S. Customs and Border Protection of DHS uses a security regime to ensure that all containers that pose a potential risk for terrorism are identified and inspected at foreign ports before they are placed on vessels destined for the United States. Ten Latin American ports in Argentina, the Bahamas, Brazil, Colombia, the Dominican Republic, Honduras, Jamaica, and Panama participate in the CSI program. The Department of Energy's National Nuclear Security Administration administers the Megaports Initiative, a program which involves deploying radiation detection equipment in order to deter, detect, and interdict illicit trafficking in nuclear and radioactive materials. To date, the Megaports Initiative is operational in ports in the Bahamas, Colombia, the Dominican Republic, Honduras, Jamaica, Mexico, and Panama.

The Department of Homeland Security's Immigration and Customs Enforcement (ICE) has partnered with several Latin American countries to establish Trade Transparency Units that facilitate exchanges of information in order to combat trade-based money laundering. TTUs have been established in Argentina, Brazil, Colombia, Paraguay, Mexico, and Panama.

Increased Regional Cooperation Since 9/11

Latin American nations strongly condemned the September 2001 terrorist attacks on the United States and took action through the OAS and the Rio Treaty to strengthen hemispheric cooperation against terrorism. The OAS, which happened to be meeting in Peru at the time, swiftly condemned the attacks, reiterated the need to strengthen hemispheric cooperation to combat terrorism, and expressed full solidarity with the United States. At a special session on September 19, 2001, OAS members invoked the 1947 Inter-American Treaty of Reciprocal Assistance, also known as the Rio Treaty, which obligates signatories to the treaty to come to one another's defense in case of outside attack. Another resolution approved on September 21, 2001, called on Rio Treaty signatories to "use all legally available measures to pursue, capture, extradite, and punish those individuals" involved in the attacks and to "render additional assistance and support to the United States, as appropriate, to address the September 11 attacks, and also to prevent future terrorist acts."

In the aftermath of 9/11, OAS members reinvigorated efforts of the of the Inter-American Committee on Terrorism (CICTE) to combat terrorism in the hemisphere. CICTE has cooperated on border security mechanisms, controls to prevent terrorist funding, and law enforcement and counterterrorism intelligence and information.[87] It has worked on a wide range of capacity building and training programs including border controls (covering maritime and aviation security, customs, and immigration), critical infrastructure protection (covering cyber security, major events security, and tourism security), counter-terrorism legislative assistance and combating terrorism financing, and strengthening strategies on emerging terrorist threats. At CICTE's 11th regular session held in March 2011, member states issued a declaration of renewed hemispheric commitment to enhance cooperation to prevent, combat, and eliminate terrorism. At CICTE's 12th regular session held in March 2012, member states focused on efforts to strengthen cyber security in the Americas. In March 2013, CICTE held its 13th regular session, member states adopted a resolution on strengthening cooperation to address terrorist financing and money laundering. At its 14th regular session held in February 2014, CICTE member focused attention on: how to counter criminal activities that may exacerbate the threat of terrorism, such as money laundering and trafficking in drugs, arms, and people; and how to strengthen criminal justice responses to acts of terrorism.

OAS members signed the Inter-American Convention Against Terrorism in June 2002. The Convention, among other measures, improves regional cooperation against terrorism, commits parties to sign and ratify U.N. anti-terrorism instruments and take actions against the financing of terrorism, and denies safe haven to suspected terrorists. President Bush submitted the Convention to the Senate on November 12, 2002, for its advice and consent, and the treaty was referred to the

---

[87] See the website of the CICTE available at http://www.cicte.oas.org/Rev/en/.

Senate Foreign Relations Committee (Treaty Doc. 107-18). In the 109th Congress, the committee formally reported the treaty on July 28, 2005 (Senate Exec. Rept. 109-3), and on October 7, 2005, the Senate agreed to the resolution of advice and consent. The United States deposited its instruments of ratification for the Convention on November 15, 2005.

Legislative Initiatives and Oversight

111th Congress

In the 111th Congress, President Obama signed into law the Comprehensive Iran Sanctions, Accountability, and Disinvestment Act of 2010 (P.L. 111-195) on July 1, 2010, which included a provision making gasoline sales to Iran subject to U.S. sanctions.

Several other measures with Venezuela provisions were considered or introduced in the 111th Congress, but action was not completed on these initiatives. In June 2010, the Senate Committee on Armed Services reported S. 3454, the National Defense Authorization Act for FY2011, with a provision that would have required a report on Venezuela related to terrorism issues. In June 2009, the House approved H.R. 2410, the Foreign Relations Authorization Act for FY2010 and FY2011, with a provision in Section 1011 that would have required a report within 90 days on Iran's and Hezbollah's actions in the Western Hemisphere. On July 23, 2009, the Senate had approved its version of the National Defense Authorization Act for FY2010, S. 1390 (Levin), with a provision that would have required the Director of National Intelligence to provide a report on Venezuela's military purchases, its potential support for the FARC and Hezbollah, and other Venezuelan activities, but the final enacted measure dropped the provision.

Other resolutions and bills related to Venezuela that were introduced in the 111th Congress included H.R. 375 (Ros-Lehtinen), introduced January 9, 2009, that would have, among its provisions, placed restrictions on nuclear cooperation with countries assisting the nuclear programs of Venezuela. H.R. 2475 (Ros-Lehtinen), introduced May 19, 2009, included a provision identical to that in H.R. 375 described above that would have placed restrictions on nuclear cooperation with countries assisting the nuclear programs of Venezuela. H.Res. 872 (Mack), introduced October 27, 2009, would have called on Venezuela to be designated a state sponsor of terrorism because of its alleged support of Iran, Hezbollah, and the FARC.

Over the years, the U.S. Congress expressed concern about progress in Argentina's investigation of the 1994 AMIA bombing, with the House often passing resolutions on the issue around the time of the anniversary of the bombing on July 18. In the 111th Congress, H.Con.Res. 156 (Ros-Lehtinen), approved July 17, 2009, again condemned the AMIA bombing and urged Western Hemisphere governments to take actions to curb the activities that support Hezbollah and other such extremist groups.

On October 27, 2009, the House Committee on Foreign Affairs, Subcommittees on the Western Hemisphere, the Middle East and South Asia, and Terrorism, Nonproliferation and Trade held a joint hearing on "Iran in the Western Hemisphere" featuring private witnesses.[88]

---

[88] A transcript and webcast of the hearing is available at http://foreignaffairs house.gov/hearing_notice.asp?id=1127.

112th Congress

The 112th Congress enacted one measure into law late in the second session, the Countering Iran in the Western Hemisphere Act of 2012 (H.R. 3783, P.L. 112-220), which requires the Administration to conduct an assessment and present "a strategy to address Iran's growing hostile presence and activity in the Western Hemisphere." Several other initiatives were introduced in the related to Mexico and Venezuela as well the activities of Iran and Hezbollah in the Western Hemisphere, but were not considered. Several oversight hearings were also held on these topics.

Mexico

Among legislative initiatives introduced, two bills, H.R. 1270 (McCaul) and H.R. 4303 (McCaul), would have directed the Secretary of State to designate as foreign terrorist organizations several Mexican drug cartels; and H.R. 3401 (Mack), the Enhanced Border Security Act, ordered reported by the House Subcommittee on the Western Hemisphere, Committee on Foreign Affairs, on December 15, 2011, would have required the Secretary of State within 90 days to submit a detailed counterinsurgency strategy "to combat the terrorist insurgency in Mexico waged by transnational criminal organizations."

Several hearings in the 112th Congress focused on the drug trafficking situation in Mexico and allegations that the drug trafficking organizations constituted a criminal insurgency or had links to terrorism. The House Committee on Foreign Affairs, Subcommittee on the Western Hemisphere, held a September 13, 2011, hearing entitled "Has Mérida Evolved? Part One: The Evolution of Drug Cartels and the Threat to Mexico's Governance" featuring private witnesses.[89] The Western Hemisphere Subcommittee followed up on October 4, 2011, with a joint hearing with the House Committee on Homeland Security, Subcommittee on Oversight, Investigations, and Management, entitled "Mérida Part Two: Insurgency and Terrorism in Mexico," with testimony from the State Department, the Drug Enforcement Administration, and the Department of Homeland Security.[90]

Looking more broadly at drug trafficking, the House Committee on Foreign Affairs, Subcommittee on Oversight and Investigations, held an October 12, 2011, hearing entitled "The International Exploitation of Drug Wars and What We Can Do About It" featuring private witnesses.[91] The House Committee on Foreign Affairs, Subcommittee on Terrorism, Nonproliferation and Trade also held two hearings on "Narcoterrorism and the Long Reach of U.S. Law Enforcement," on October 12 and November 17, 2011, that examined the links between drug trafficking and terrorism worldwide and featured private witnesses and an official from the Drug Enforcement Administration.[92]

---

[89] A transcript and webcast of the hearing is available at http://foreignaffairs house.gov/hearing_notice.asp?id=1348.

[90] Testimony and a webcast of the joint hearing is available at http://homeland.house.gov/hearing/joint-subcommittee-hearing-m%C3%A9rida-part-two-insurgency-and-terrorism-mexico.

[91] A transcript and webcast of the hearing is available at http://foreignaffairs house.gov/hearing_notice.asp?id=1365.

[92] A transcript and webcast of the October 12, 2001, hearing is available at http://foreignaffairs.house.gov/hearing_notice.asp?id=1362; a webcast of the November 17, 2011, hearing is available at http://foreignaffairs.house.gov/hearing_notice.asp?id=1379.

Venezuela

H.Res. 247 (Mack) would have condemned Venezuela "for its state-sponsored support of international terrorist groups" and called "on the Secretary of State to designate Venezuela as a state sponsor of terrorism" for "its support of Iran, Hezbollah, and the Revolutionary Armed Forces of Colombia (FARC)."

On June 24, 2011, a joint hearing on "Venezuela's Sanctionable Activities" by subcommittees of the House Committee on Foreign Affairs and the House Committee on Oversight and Government Reform featured testimony by State Department and Treasury Department officials. State Department officials expressed concern about "Venezuela's relations with Iran, its support for the FARC, [and] its lackluster cooperation on counterterrorism."[93] Administration officials testified that Hezbollah's activity in Venezuela was confined to fundraising.

Iran and Hezbollah in the Western Hemisphere

As noted above, Congress completed action on H.R. 3783 (Duncan), the Countering Iran in the Western Hemisphere Act of 2012, in December 2012 and the measure was signed into law on December 28, 2012 (P.L. 112-220). As enacted, the measure requires the Secretary of State to conduct an assessment within 180 days of the "threats posed to the United States by Iran's growing presence and activity in the Western Hemisphere" and a strategy to address these threats. The required strategy may be submitted in classified form, but shall include an unclassified summary of policy recommendations to address the growing Iranian threat in the Western Hemisphere. The bill also states that "it shall be the policy of the United States to use a comprehensive government-wide strategy to counter Iran's growing hostile presence and activity in the Western Hemisphere by working together with United States allies and partners in the region to mutually deter threats to United States interests by the Government of Iran, the Iranian Islamic Revolutionary Guards Corps (IRGC), the IRGC's Qods Force, and Hezbollah."

Several other legislative initiatives were introduced, but not considered, in the 112th Congress. H.Res. 429 (Duncan), introduced in the first session, would have called for the Administration to include the Western Hemisphere in its 2012 National Strategy for Counterterrorism's Area of Focus, with specific attention on the "counterterrorism threat to the homeland emanating from Iran's growing presence and activity in the Western Hemisphere." A much broader bill, H.R. 6067 (Ros-Lehtinen), the Western Hemisphere Security Cooperation Act of 2012, introduced in the second session, included a number of provisions designed to counter Iranian and Hezbollah activities in the Western Hemisphere and several other broader provisions promoting Western Hemisphere cooperation on terrorism.

Several hearings were held in the 112th Congress dealing with concerns about Iran and Hezbollah in Latin America. In the first session, the House Committee on Homeland Security, Subcommittee on Counterterrorism and Intelligence held a July 7, 2011, hearing on "Hezbollah in Latin

---

[93] Joint Hearing on "Venezuela's Sanctionable Activities," House Committee on Foreign Affairs, Subcommittee on the Western Hemisphere and Subcommittee on the Middle East and South Asia, and House Committee on Oversight and Government Reform, Subcommittee on National Security, Homeland Defense and Foreign Operations. June 24, 2011. Testimony and webcast of the joint hearing is available at http://oversight.house.gov/index.php?option=com_content&view=article&id=1349%3A6-24-11-qvenezuelas-sanctionable-activityq&catid=17&Itemid=25.

America—Implications for U.S. Policy," featuring private witnesses.[94] The joint June 24, 2011, hearing by the House Committees on Foreign Affairs and on Oversight and Government Reform on "Venezuela's Sanctionable Activities" cited above also touched on concerns about Iran and Hezbollah in the Western Hemisphere. The House Foreign Affairs Committee held a broader hearing on October 13, 2011, entitled "Emerging Threats and Security in the Western Hemisphere: Next Steps for U.S. Policy," with witnesses from the Departments of State, Treasury, and Defense that touched on concerns about Iran and Hezbollah in the Western Hemisphere.[95]

In the second session, hearings were held in both houses. The House Foreign Affairs Committee held a February 2, 2012, hearing focused on Iranian President Ahmadinejad's January 2012 trip to Latin America.[96] The Senate Foreign Relations Committee's Subcommittee on Western Hemisphere, Peace Corps, and Global Narcotics Affairs held a February 16, 2012, hearing on Iran's influence and activity in Latin America.[97] The House Committee on Homeland Security, Subcommittee on Oversight, Investigations, and Management held a hearing on November 16, 2012, assessing threats to U.S. borders. The subcommittee updated a majority staff report that it had issued in 2006 examining violence at the Southwest border, which included a section looking at the activities of Iran and Hezbollah in Latin America. Private witnesses at the hearing alleged extensive activities of both Iran and Hezbollah in the region.[98]

113th Congress

To date in the 113th Congress, several hearings have been held that focus or touch upon the role of Iran and Hezbollah in Latin America and two legislative initiatives on Cuba have been introduced related to U.S. fugitives from justice and the state sponsor of terrorism list.

The House Committee on Foreign Affairs, Subcommittee on Terrorism, Nonproliferation and Trade held a March 20, 2013, hearing on Hezbollah as a global terrorist threat with private witnesses. The hearing included testimony by former State Department Assistant Secretary for Western Hemisphere Affairs Roger Noriega alleging extensive Hezbollah activities in at least a dozen countries in Latin America, especially Venezuela, and involvement in criminal and terrorist activity in the region.[99]

---

[94] U.S. Congress, House Committee on Homeland Security, Subcommittee on Counterterrorism and Intelligence, "Hezbollah in Latin America—Implications for U.S. Homeland Security," July 7, 2011. Testimony and webcast available at http://homeland house.gov/hearing/subcommittee-hearing-hezbollah-latin-america-implications-us-homeland-security.

[95] A transcript and webcast of the hearing is available at http://foreignaffairs house.gov/hearing_notice.asp?id=1361.

[96] A webcast of the hearing is available at http://foreignaffairs house.gov/hearing_notice.asp?id=1396.

[97] Testimony and a webcast of the hearing is available at http://www foreign.senate.gov/hearings/irans-influence-and-activity-in-latin-america.

[98] U.S. Congress, House Committee on Homeland Security, Subcommittee on Oversight, Investigations, and Management, Hearing, "A Line in the Sand: Assessing Dangerous Threats to Our Nation's Borders," November 16, 2013, available at http://homeland house.gov/hearing/subcommittee-hearing-line-sand-assessing-dangerous-threats-our-nation%E2%80%99s-borders.

[99] U.S. Congress, House Committee on Foreign Affairs, Subcommittee on Terrorism, Nonproliferation and Trade, Hearing on "Hezbollah's Strategic Shift: A Global Terrorist Threat," March 20, 2013, available at http://foreignaffairs.house.gov/hearing/subcommittee-hearing-hezbollah%E2%80%99s-strategic-shift-global-terrorist-threat.

On March 12, 2013, the Senate Select Committee on Intelligence held an open hearing on security threats to the United States. Director of National Intelligence James Clapper testified that Iran has cultivated ties with the leaders of Bolivia, Cuba, Ecuador, Nicaragua, and Venezuela, and that Iran's relations with the governments of these countries offers a way for them "to stake out independent positions on the international issue of Iran, while extracting financial aid and investment for economic and social projects."[100]

On March 19 and 20, 2013, the Senate and House Armed Services Committees, respectively, held oversight hearings on SOUTHCOM, in which Commander General John F. Kelly presented the command's 2013 posture statement. With regard to Iran's activities in the Western Hemisphere, General Kelly stated: "The reality of the ground is that Iran is struggling to maintain influence in the region, and that its efforts to cooperate with a small set of countries with interests that are inimical to the United States are waning." General Kelly further stated that "the Iranian regime has increased its diplomatic and economic outreach across the region with nations like Venezuela, Bolivia, Ecuador, and Argentina," but that the "outreach has only been marginally successful ... and the region as a whole has not been receptive to Iranian efforts." With regard to Hezbollah, General Kelly reported in the posture statement that members and supporters of Hezbollah have an established presence in several countries in the region, and that the Lebanese Shi'a diaspora in the region may generate as much as tens of millions of dollars for Hezbollah through licit and illicit means. More broadly, General Kelly raised the question of the possible nexus between international terrorist organizations and criminal networks. He noted the 2011 Iranian plot to assassinate the Saudi Ambassador to the United States as a demonstration of Iran's willingness to leverage criminal groups to carry out its objectives in the U.S. homeland.[101]

On July 9, 2013, the House Homeland Security Committee, Subcommittee on Oversight and Management Efficiency, held a hearing on Iran's influence in the Western Hemisphere. The hearing included several private witnesses contending that Iran's influence in the region has grown, contrary to a finding in the State Department's June 27, 2013, report to Congress that Iran's influence in the region is waning. Another witness maintained that Iran's efforts in the region to date have met with mixed results, but also contended that the ebb of Iran's economic activity in the region resulting from increased international sanctions could make Iran more desperate to find willing trading partners in the region.[102]

On August 1, 2013, two subcommittees of the House Foreign Affairs Committee—the Subcommittee on the Middle East and North Africa, and the Subcommittee on the Western Hemisphere—held a joint hearing examining the State Department's report on Iran's presence in the Western Hemisphere. The hearing included several private witnesses, two of whom criticized the State Department's report on Iran in the Western Hemisphere, and another witness who

---

[100] James R. Clapper, Director of National Intelligence, "Worldwide Threat Assessment of the US Intelligence .Community," Statement for the Record, Senate Select Committee on Intelligence, March 12, 2013, available at http://intelligence.senate.gov/130312/clapper.pdf.

[101] General John F. Kelly, Commander, United States Southern Command, Posture Statement, Senate Armed Services Committee, March 19, 2013, available at http://www.armed-services.senate.gov/statemnt/2013/03%20March/ Kelly%2003-19-13.pdf.

[102] U.S. Congress, House Committee on Homeland Security, Subcommittee on Oversight and Management Efficiency, *Threat to the Homeland: Iran's Extending Influence in the Western Hemisphere*, Hearing, July 9, 2013, available at http://homeland house.gov/hearing/subcommittee-hearing-threat-homeland-iran%E2%80%99s-extending-influence-western-hemisphere

stressed that even if the State Department assessment was accurate, that the United States still needed to continue being watchful about the activities of both Iran and Hezbollah in the region.[103]

In the second session of the 113th Congress, on February 4, 2014, the House Committee on Foreign Affairs, Subcommittee on Terrorism, Nonproliferation, and Trade, held a hearing on "Terrorist Groups in Latin America: The Changing Landscape." The hearing focused on efforts to combat the Shining Path in Peru and FARC in Colombia, as well as concerns about the activities of Hezbollah in the region.[104]

The House Armed Services Committee held a hearing on SOUTCHOM's 2014 posture statement on February 26, 2014, while the Senate Armed Services Committee held a similar hearing on March 13, 2014. General John Kelly testified that he remains concerned that Hezbollah "maintains an operations presence" in the region and stated that "Islamic extremists visit the region to proselytize, recruit, establish business venues to generate funds, and expand their radical networks."[105]

With regard to legislative initiatives introduced in the 113th Congress, H.R. 1917 (Rush), introduced May 9, 2013, would among its provisions rescind any determination of the Secretary of State in effect on the date of enactment of the Act that Cuba has repeatedly provided support for acts of international terrorism. H.Res. 262 (King), introduced June 14, 2013, would call for the immediate extradition or rendering to the United States of convicted felon William Morales and all fugitives from justice who are receiving safe harbor in Cuba in order to escape prosecution or confinement for criminal offenses in the United States.

Conclusion

For most countries in Latin America and the Caribbean, threats emanating from terrorism are low. The majority of terrorist acts in the region is perpetrated by the Revolutionary Armed Forces of Colombia. According to the Department of State, while Latin American governments have made modest improvements to their counterterrorism capabilities, more significant progress has been limited by several factors, including corruption, weak governmental institutions, insufficient interagency cooperation, weak or nonexistent legislation, and a lack of resources. Both Cuba and Venezuela are on the State Department's list of countries determined to be not cooperating fully with U.S. antiterrorism efforts, and Cuba has remained on the State Department's list of state sponsors of terrorism since 1982. U.S. officials and some Members of Congress have expressed concern over the past several years about the activities of Iran and Hezbollah in Latin America. There is disagreement, however, over the extent and significance of Iran's activities in Latin America. A June 2013 State Department report to Congress maintained that Iran's influence in the

---

[103] U.S. Congress, House Committee on Foreign Affairs, Subcommittee on Middle East and North Africa and Subcommittee on the Western Hemisphere, *Examining the State Department's Report on Iranian Presence in the Western Hemisphere 1 Years After Its Att...*, Joint Hearing, 113th Cong., 1st sess., August 1, 2013, Serial No. 113-65 (Washington: GPO, 2013).

[104] U.S. Congress, House Committee on Foreign Affairs, Subcommittee on Terrorism, Nonproliferation, and Trade, *Terrorist Groups in Latin America: The Changing Landscape*, Hearing, 113th Cong., 2nd sess., February 4, 2014, Serial No. 113-121 (Washington: GPO, 2014).

[105] Posture Statement of General John F. Kelly, Commander, U.S. Southern Command, before the 113th Congress, House Armed Services Committee, February 26, 2014, available at: http://www.southcom.mil/newsroom/Documents/2014_SOUTHCOM_Posture_Statement_HASC_FINAL_PDF.pdf

region is waning. Some critics maintain that the State Department is playing down the threat posed by Iranian activities in the region, while others who agree with the assessment of the State Department maintain that Iranian activities in the region, while a concern, are being exaggerated. The State Department maintains that there are no known operational cells of either Al Qaeda or Hezbollah-related groups in the hemisphere, although it notes that ideological sympathizers continue to provide financial and ideological support to these and other terrorist groups in the Middle East and South Asia.

Author Contact Information

Mark P. Sullivan
Specialist in Latin American Affairs
msullivan@crs.loc.gov, 7-7689

June S. Beittel
Analyst in Latin American Affairs
jbeittel@crs.loc.gov, 7-7613